The Millionaire and the Scrublady and Other Parables

William E. Barton

The
Millionaire
and the
Scrublady

and
Other Parables

William E. Barton

EDITED BY

Garth Rosell and Stan Flewelling

Broadmoor BOOKS
Zondervan Publishing House
Grand Rapids, Michigan

The Millionaire and the Scrublady and Other Parables
Copyright © 1990 by Garth Rosell and Stan Flewelling

Broadmoor Books are published by
Zondervan Publishing House
1415 Lake Drive, S.E.,
Grand Rapids, Michigan 49506

Library of Congress Cataloging in Publication Data

Barton, William Eleazar, 1861–1930.
    The millionaire and the scrublady and other parables / William E.
  Barton : edited by Garth Rosell and Stan Flewelling.
      p. cm.
    ISBN 0-310-39651-4
    1. Christian life — Congregationalist authors. 2. Parables.
I. Rosell, Garth. II. Flewelling, Stan. III. Title.
BV4515.2.B29 1990
242 — dc20   90 – 35572
                                                          CIP

Printed in the United States of America

90 91 92 93 94 95 / CH / 10 9 8 7 6 5 4 3 2 1

For our Parents
Mervin and Violette
William and Esther

Contents

Preface

Nearly a decade has passed since Bob Dvorak, my good friend and former colleague, first introduced me to the wonderful stories of William E. Barton. Despite their age, Barton's little parables immediately captivated me with their rare blend of freshness, spiritual insight, and charm. Before long I was a devoted disciple.

It took me nearly five years, however, to track down a complete set of the stories. Although 326 of them were published in book form between 1917 and 1925, the five volumes which make up this set are not only long out of print but they are also quite difficult to find even in used book stores with extensive holdings.

As I began to share the stories with my friends — around the dinner table, in the pulpit, and in the class-room — I discovered that nearly everyone, old and young alike, welcomed them as enthusiastically as I had. When requests for copies began to follow virtually every reading, it became apparent that some means had to be found to make them more widely available to readers of our generation.

My growing interest in helping to put together a new edition of the stories was further strengthened when Stan

Flewelling offered to join me on the project. With the encouragement of Ed Van der Maas, who himself fell under the spell of Barton's parables around our dining room table, Stan and I approached Zondervan Publishing House to see if they might be interested in producing such a volume. Not only did they agree to publish a new edition of the parables, but John Sloan, Bob Hudson, and their excellent staff colleagues have provided the technical and editorial expertise which were needed to bring the project to completion.

Many others have helped us as well. Special thanks are due to the members of William E. Barton's family, whose support for the project made it possible for us to proceed. We want to express our appreciation also to Mary Jasper Cate and Lexie Kirkpatrick whose skill, hard work, and practical encouragement were so important to the completion of our task. For all of us, it was a labor of love.

— Dr. Garth Rosell

Introduction

The longest entry in the 1930 edition of *Who's Who in America* was the one devoted to William E. Barton, pastor, author, and lecturer. It described his productive and versatile life, a life that would soon come to an end. Subsequent eulogies in the secular press focused on Barton's meticulous biographical work on Abraham Lincoln. Much of the Christian community, however, was especially saddened over the loss of "Safed the Sage," Barton's alter ego who had emerged in a series of tales he called modern-day parables.

Born in the village of Sublette, Illinois, in 1861, William Barton was the eldest son of a country doctor turned druggist and postmaster. Determined to get a good education, young Barton took odd jobs, attended a preparatory school, and in 1881 enrolled at Berea College, a Congregational school in the Kentucky hills notable both then and now for its work-study programs. At Berea, Barton acquired a reputation as one of the school's most gregarious and mischievous students.

Esther Bushnell came to Berea in 1883 from her parents' Ohio farm. She taught in the primary model school of the education department and met William Barton on the annual "Mountain Excursion" picnic. By the end of the school year they were engaged.

William and Esther spent hours together hiking and riding horseback in the hills around Berea, particularly "The Pinnacle" that overlooks the town from the east. Years later on a sentimental whim, they bought the whole mountain, in time bequeathing it to the college. Today the twin-bluff peak of the hill is still known as "Barton's Knob." *The Pinnacle* is the student newspaper.

Barton majored in law. A few weeks before graduation, the American Missionary Association offered him an assignment in the nearby Appalachian hills. Barton felt called to work in the mountains, where he'd already spent summers teaching public school and getting to know the people. He wasn't so sure about a call to the ministry, so he sought the advice of those who knew him best. The unanimous encouragement he received from his parents, professors, and most of all his fiancée, was overwhelming.

So it was that in the summer of 1885, Barton was ordained by the Congregational Church, awarded the first of many degrees, and married to Esther Bushnell.

The Bartons moved to Robbins, Tennessee, the hub of a preaching circuit William soon developed. He gathered twenty-seven small congregations in settlements with names like Deer Lodge, Brimstone Creek, and Helenwood.

When the Bartons' first child was born (and they took on the added responsibility of two abandoned black children whom they had brought into their home as well), William knew he would need to supplement his meager preacher's salary. So he took up writing. His earliest works characterized the folks around him whose ways of life he had come to appreciate. He was one of the first collectors of mountain hymns and spirituals.

After two years in Tennessee, Barton felt it was time for full theological training. He moved his growing family to Ohio where he attended Oberlin Seminary and was valedictorian of the class of 1890. He pastored two nearby village churches before being called to the prominent Shawmut Church in Boston.

Barton's friends in the "Jerusalem" of American Congregationalism were as famous — and different — as Edward Everett Hale, Unitarian "first citizen" of the city, and Dwight L. Moody, who came to Boston for evangelistic services. He treated them all with respect. In turn, his peers and his congregation grew to love and revere him.

They especially noted Barton's gift for bridging gaps others spent their energy widening. He used to quote an aging New Hampshire pastor whom he'd asked, "What have you learned in the long years of your ministry that would modify your methods if you were to begin life again?" "This," the pastor answered, "that there is more to be said on the other side of almost any question than I once supposed."

In 1899 Barton received a call from the First Congregational Church of Oak Park, Illinois. He accepted, and stayed until his retirement twenty-five years later. In his parish were the families of prominent Chicago business leaders, state legislators, pastors emeriti, and briefly, a young Ernest Hemingway. When Barton arrived, First Church was deeply divided and in debt. By the time he left, it was dubbed the western "cathedral of Congregationalism."

If the church was a cathedral, Barton was archbishop. Beyond the demands of his own congregation there was no shortage of boards and societies he was asked to join and often lead. He was a trustee of three schools, a delegate to national and international conferences. The Congregational National Council chose him moderator for 1921–23.

Meanwhile, Esther was the quiet pillar of their busy home, raising four sons and a daughter, and other children they took in from time to time. She was active in Missions organizations, regularly contributing to needy causes close to home and abroad.

Somehow William Barton maintained his prolific writing. He edited several periodicals, contributed to others, and authored over sixty volumes. At home in the "Land of Lincoln," he produced twelve books and numerous articles on the life of the great president. His collection of Lincoln materials was one of the finest in the country. Renowned in his day as the biographer most able to understand Lincoln's early years, Barton is considered "one of the last of the great amateur historians."

But Barton's most popular works were his parables of Safed and Keturah.

The parables first appeared in 1915. Barton was editing *The Advance,* the religious weekly that nineteen years earlier had introduced Charles M. Sheldon's *In His Steps* as a serial feature. When Barton took over, the periodical was floundering and expected to fold.

Short on funds, Barton invested considerable resources of his own as he nursed *The Advance* back to health. Short on copy, he wrote much of it himself. For variety, he tried new literary styles, sometimes using a pseudonym for a newly created column. "My father's great-grandfather had no further use for his name," he revealed years later. So "Rev. Jacob Bostedo, D.D." got the byline for a series of Bible studies.

The concept of Safed the Sage "came" to Barton when he and Esther were on a vacation trip. He witnessed an incident that struck him as a metaphor of the ministry. Using the archaic language of an ancient storyteller, he ran the anecdote in *The Advance* as "A Parable of Safed the Sage."

Apparently it was a genre Barton enjoyed. Parables appeared regularly for the next four months. Then a letter arrived saying they were "undignified and unworthy" of the paper. Barton dropped the column, thinking he'd made a mistake.

Within a week of Safed's disappearance, however, a storm of correspondence blew in. "Has the Sage been 'fired'?" asked an anxious admirer. There were litanies of praise: "shrewd insight into human nature," "a rare combination of sanity and 'pep,'" "nearer to the heart of things than many profound treatises on theology." One family read Safed each week at the breakfast table "with mingled enjoyment and profit." Another pasted Safed's clippings in a scrapbook and shared them with neighbors.

So an encouraged Barton resumed the parables, and they kept "coming" for the remainder of his life, fifteen years in all.

The first anthology was compiled in 1917 at the request of First Church members and *Advance* subscribers. Only a thousand copies of *The Parables of Safed the Sage* were printed.

By now Safed had introduced several kinfolk who were regulars in his cast of characters: "Keturah, the wife of my bosom" and "the daughter of the daughter of Keturah," who, as all readers knew, was "unto me as the Apple of mine Eye." Later the "Little Brother and Little Sister of the daughter of the daughter of Keturah" arrived in real life and made their debuts. They were the three children of Clyde and Helen Barton Stilwell, who lived near the parsonage.

Also in 1917 *The Advance* merged with a larger denominational weekly, *The Congregationalist,* and Safed was discovered by a wider audience. Here, among doctrinal essays and bits of church news, were whimsical tales of a family finding lessons in common daily experiences. They were fun and quotable.

Soon other religious periodicals, including *The Christian Century,* picked up syndication. By the early 1920s, Safed was said to have a following of at least three million. Four more book collections were completed: *The Wit and Wisdom of Safed the Sage* (1919), *Safed and Keturah* (1921), *More Parables of Safed the Sage* (1923), and *Fun and Philosophy of Safed the Sage* (1925). Translations were distributed in Europe.

Turning an ordinary event into an illustration of spiritual truth was always a keynote of Barton's ministry style. "All true teaching is parabolic," he used to say. "We learn by using familiar things as a kind of yardstick with which to measure things less familiar. . . . If there were more parabolic teaching, there would be less dull and more effective preaching."

But, quipped Barton, Safed "never intended to pose as a preacher. . . . [He] is a philosopher rather than a priest, and finds his pulpit wherever he meets men and women and little children." This philosopher was likably invested with "a little mystery and Oriental drapery," and plenty of horse sense.

The name of the sage (pronounced SAY-fed by the Bartons) wasn't meant to be mysterious. Barton wanted an aura to his character that would distinguish him from the familiar wise men of traditional literature. Quite spontaneously he adopted the name of an Arab village in northern Galilee long regarded as the "city on a hill [which] cannot be hidden" (Matthew 5:14 NIV).

Photographers caught a consistent solemnity in Barton's face, rarely a smile. He wore a public dignity that obscured the twinkle lurking deep within his discerning eyes. As he aged, his dark hair and carefully groomed Vandyke turned fully white, making him look all the more like the sage he portrayed in print.

In contrast to William, Esther shunned the limelight. The light that found her and brought national recognition to her literary role as Keturah, Safed's enduring spouse, continually surprised her. But in their home relationship she was no limited partner. "She is a Wise Woman," her sheepish husband would say when she found him tangled in a bit of foolishness, "and when she hath Laughed, she doth not Rub It In." Few who read his stories could miss the profound mutual respect that Safed and Keturah held for each other.

Safed enjoyed all of Barton's favorite pastimes. He was a gardener — who spared dandelions ("My first Ancestor was a Gardener, and he could not Hold Down his Job"). He loved to eat ("I can digest anything save it be Health Foods"). He traveled extensively, preferring the sociability of trains to the convenience of cars (Barton's on-the-road philosophy: "I do not assume responsibility for running the train. . . . So travel does not tire me as much as it tires some people").

Like Aesop before him, Safed found lessons in nature, but people were his real motivation. Through him readers saw the vulnerable side of a notable man of God, the inspiration and imperfection of his home. The stories told more about the Bartons' private life than anything published before his posthumous *Autobiography*. That work was first serialized in the *Christian Herald* and was introduced by the Bartons' eldest son, Bruce, an advertising executive and inspirational writer whose own bestsellers far outsold his father's. Exclaimed the *Herald*, "Unquestionably this is one of the greatest features we have ever run." Another periodical reviewed the *Autobiography* under the headline, "The Story of Safed the Sage," demonstrating how closely its readers associated the late pastor and the philosopher.

Barton retired from the ministry in 1924. Early the following year, though she was not well, Esther accompanied William on an around-the-world voyage, the gift of their grateful church. At every port of call where Americans lived, he said, "there were those who waited to waft a welcome to 'Keturah' before the ship came to dock." A hospital in China and a mission assembly hall in India already bore her name.

When the tour ended, William and Esther settled at

21

their summer home in Foxboro, Massachusetts. It was the "Eden" where generations of Bartons had been reunited and refreshed since 1895, a site the family heirs continued to enjoy until it was acquired by the state park system in 1985. Within five months of their return, Esther Barton died of heart failure. Hundreds of letters and telegrams poured in to the family from around the country. President and Mrs. Coolidge sent flowers and condolences. The parables continued, but as her husband put it, "something very precious went out of them."

Five years later when William Barton also succumbed to heart problems, *The Christian Century* lamented, "Who can take the place of Safed the Sage? . . . As commentaries on the ever-changing, yet changeless comedie humaine those parables have been unsurpassed." Indeed, nothing quite like them has come along since.

— *Stan Flewelling*

The Millionaire
and the Scrublady
and Other Parables

The Millionaire
and
the Scrublady

There is a certain Millionaire, who hath his Offices on the Second Floor of the First National Bank Building. And when he goeth up to his Offices he rideth in the Elevator, but when he goeth down, then he walketh.

And he is an Haughty Man, who once was poor, and hath risen in the World. He is a Self-made Man who worshipeth his maker.

And he payeth his Rent regularly on the first day of the month, and he considereth not that there are Human Beings who run the Elevators, and who Clean the Windows, hanging at a great height above the Sidewalk, and who shovel Coal into the furnaces under the Boilers. Neither doth he at Christmas time remember any of them with a Tip or a Turkey.

And there is in that Building a Poor Woman who Scrubbeth the Stairs and the Halls. And he hath walked past her often but hath never seen her until Recently. For his head was high in the air, and he was thinking of More Millions.

Now it came to pass on a day that he left his Office, and started to walk down the Stairs.

And the Scrublady was half way down; for she had

begun at the top, and was giving the stairs their First Onceover. And upon the topmost Stair, in a wet and soapy spot, there was a Large Cake of Yellow Soap. And the Millionaire stepped upon it.

Now the foot which he set upon the Soap flew eastward toward the Sunrise, and the other foot started on an expedition of its own toward the going down of the Sun. And the Millionaire sat down upon the Topmost Step, but he did not remain there. As it had been his Intention to Descend, so he Descended, but not in the manner of his Original Design. And as he descended he struck each step with a sound as if it had been a Drum.

And the Scrublady stood aside courteously, and let him go.

And at the bottom he arose, and considered whether he should rush into the Office of the Building and demand that the Scrublady be fired; but he considered that if he should tell the reason there would be great Mirth among the occupants of the Building. And so he held his peace.

But since that day he taketh notice of the Scrublady, and passeth her with Circumspection.

For there is no one so high or mighty that he can afford to ignore any of his fellow human beings. For a very Humble Scrublady and a very common bar of Yellow Soap can take the mind of a Great Man off his Business Troubles with surprising rapidity.

Wherefore, consider these things, and count not thyself too high above even the humblest of the children of God.

Lest haply thou come down from thy place of pride and walk off with thy bruises aching a little more by reason of thy suspicion that the Scrublady is Smiling into her Suds, and facing the day's work the more cheerfully by reason of the fun thou hast afforded her.

For these are solemn days, and he that bringeth a smile to the face of a Scrublady hath not lived in vain. ❧

The Mystery
of the Hole

Now I entered the Kitchen, and would have passed through. But Keturah was there; so I waited: and she cast Divers Things into a Great Bowl, and did stir them with a Great Spoon.

And I asked her, saying, What hast thou in the Bowl?

And she said, Sugar and Spice, and all that's nice.

And I said, That is what God used when He made thee.

And she took the Dough out of the Bowl, when she had stirred it, and she rolled it with a Rolling-Pin; and she cut it into round cakes. And in the midst of every several cake was there an Hole. And a great Caldron hung above the Fire, and there was Fat therein and it boiled furiously.

And Keturah took the round Cakes of Dough, and cast them into the Caldron; and she poked them with a Fork, and she turned them, and when they came forth, behold I knew then what they were. And the smell of them was inviting, and the appearance of them was exceeding good. And Keturah gave me one of the Doughnuts, and Believe Me, they were Some Doughnuts.

And I said, To what purpose is the Hole? If the

Doughnut be so good with a part Punched Out, how much better had it been if the Hole also had been Doughnut!

And Keturah answered and said, Thou speakest as a Fool, who is never content with the Goodness that is, but always complaineth against God for the lack of the Goodness which he thinketh is not. If there were no Hole in the Doughnut, then were it like unto Ephraim, a cake not turned. For, though the Cake were Fried till the Edges thereof were burnt and hard as thy Philosopher's Stone, yet would there be uncooked Dough in the middle. Yea, thou shouldest then break thy teeth on the outer rim of every Several Doughnut, and the middle part thereof would be Raw Dough.

And I meditated much on what Keturah had told me. And I considered the Empty Spaces in Human life; and the Desolation of its Vacancies; and how hearts break over its Blank Interstices. And I pondered in my soul whether God doth not know that save for these our lives would be like unto Ephraim.

And I spake of these things to Keturah, and she said, I know not the secret of these mysteries. Yea, mine own heart acheth over some of the Empty Places. But say unto those who are able to hear that the person who useth not the good things which he hath but complaineth against God for those he lacketh, is like unto one who rejecteth a Doughnut because he Knoweth not the Mystery of the Hole. ❧

HPB Outlet Ohio
2231 Westbelt Dr.
Columbus, OH 43228
UNITED STATES
outletohio@hpb.com

HPB Outlet Ohio
2231 Westbelt Dr.
Columbus, OH 43228
UNITED STATES

To: Virginia Birks
4894 Robertsville Ave., SE
East Canton, OH 44730
UNITED STATES

Marketplace:	Amazon US
Order Number:	1763965
Ship Method:	Standard
Customer Name:	Virginia Birks
Order Date:	8/12/2012
Marketplace Order #:	104-0012952-7337875
Email:	2fcwrqy66h6pmrb@marketplace.amazon.com

Items:

1 William Eleazar Barton
SKU: mon000007878764
ISBN: 0310396514 - Books

L01-2-75-018-001-388

Good

$0.46

Subtotal: $0.46
Shipping: $3.99

Total: $4.45

Notes:

Thanks for your order!

If you have any questions or concerns regarding this order, please contact us at outletohio@hpb.com

Things
That Are Small

I was putting on my Outer Garments, and going unto a Committee Meeting. And I was late. And Keturah said unto me, Go thou by the way of the house of our Daughter, and give unto her this Package, and speak unto her such and such Messages, and then go thou unto thy Committee Meeting.

And I did even as she said unto me. But I was in haste, and I tarried not long, nor sat down.

And as I hastened away, I heard a great Cry, and I turned back to see if the daughter of the daughter of Keturah had broken her Neck. And she had not broken her Neck, but I had broken her Heart.

And I asked, What is the matter with my little girl?

And she sobbed and she answered, Grandpa hardly spoke to me. Am I so little he does not care for me?

Now when I heard this I was smitten to mine heart, for it had been even as she said. And the little maiden is unto me as the Apple of mine Eye. But I had been in an Hurry, for there was a Committee Meeting, and I was late.

And I entered the House, and I took her into mine arms, and I sat in a Chair with the little maiden in my lap, and with her Golden Hair upon my Shoulder, and I said, Let the Committee Meeting go hang.

And she said, Do you love me, Grandpa, even if I am small?

And I said, My dear, I love thee as much as if thou wert an Elephant in the Circus, and maybe more. Yea, I do not think it would be possible for a Grandsire to love a little damsel more than I love thee.

And she put her arms around my neck, and the Committee Meeting just had to mosey along as best it could till I got there.

Now after a while she got down, and we bade each other an Happy Good-bye, and I went my way. And as I went, I thought of the children of God who sometimes get to feeling just the same way, and thinking that their Heavenly Father doth not care for them because they are so Little, and He is busy with Great Things.

And I prayed unto my God on behalf of all such Heart-Broken children of His, that He will gather them in his arms, and comfort them, and tell them to cast all their care upon Him, for it Mattereth to Him concerning them.

No Gum in Goodness

I spake unto Keturah, saying, I must take me unto the shop of the Barber.

Now the daughter of the daughter of Keturah was there, and she spake unto me, saying, Grandpa, the Barber giveth unto every one that hath his hair cut a Stick of Gum. Wilt thou bring the Gum unto me?

And I answered and said unto her,

Alas, my little maiden, it cannot be. Youth hath many privileges which belong not unto those advanced in years, and among them is the privilege of receiving Gum from the Barber. If there come unto the shop of the Barber a nice little girl, and she sitteth very quietly in his chair while he bobbeth her hair just below her ears, unto her doth he give a Stick of Gum. And peradventure there come unto his shop a Small Boy, and he maketh no fuss, but remaineth quietly in the chair, and goeth forth smiling, with his hair cut just as short as mine, unto him also doth the Barber give a Stick of Gum. But unto aged men like unto thy Grandpa doth he give no Gum, yea, though they be never so good. Rejoice in thy youth, and congratulate thyself that thou hast entered into the Kingdom of heaven as a little child. For youth there is a balm in Gilead, but for Grandpa there is no Gum in Goodness.

And she said, Grandpa, across the street from the shop of the Barber is a Drug Store. And in the Drug Store there is Gum. Howbeit, they give thee not one stick but five, and thou shalt give unto the man in the white coat a Nickel.

And I said, Between one stick which the Barber giveth free and five sticks which the man with the white coat in the Drug Store giveth for a nickel, is a measurable difference in good hard Cash.

And she waited a moment, and she said, Grandpa, wilt thou bring me the Gum?

And I said, Perhaps.

And she considered, and she asked, saying, Grandpa, what is the meaning of "Perhaps"?

And I said, the word Perhaps is a word of widely different connotations. For sometimes it meaneth, Not if I can think of some good reason for not doing it. And again it meaneth, It shall never be done.

And she said, Grandpa, what doth Perhaps mean when a little girl asketh her Grandpa for Gum and she asketh him very nicely and sayeth Please?

And I said, It meaneth that she shall have the Gum.

And she got it.

Now Keturah heard all this, and she said nothing, but I saw her smiling as though the little maiden were learning some things which her grandmother knew a long time ago.

And I said unto Keturah, I wonder if I could write a Parable about the different meanings of a word?

And Keturah said, Perhaps. ❧

The
Strawberry Sundae

I went unto the Shop where they sell Books; for I desired to buy a Book. And the daughter of the daughter of Keturah went with me. And we rode together on the Trolley Cars, and we had a good time.

And when we came to the place where they sell Books, then did I show her a Picture Book while I looked over the New Books. And I bought one or two.

And when we departed, she said unto me, Grandpa, wilt thou buy for me an Ice Cream Cone?

And I said, I will surely do so; and if thou shalt say, Please, then will I do even better.

And she said, Please.

And we came unto a place where they sell Sweets, and we went within.

And I said, Shall I buy for thee a Sundae?

And she said, I have never eaten a Sundae, but I should like it very much.

And I said, What flavor wilt thou have?

And she said, I desire Chocolate.

So I bought for her a Chocolate Sundae, but as for myself, I bought Strawberry. For I think the Strawberry is the next to the best Berry that the Lord ever made (the best being the Red Raspberry, which I like much).

So the little maiden ate her Chocolate Sundae, and liked it exceeding well. But she liked the Ripe, Rich, Red, Juicy Color of my Strawberry. So that she looked over now and then and almost wished that she had not ordered Chocolate. And when I saw that she was Interested, I ate slowly, so that when she had finished, I had only begun. And that was Rather Hard upon the little maiden.

Now, when she had finished, she clasped her little hands together, and she leaned her little round elbows on the table, and she rested her chin on her little clasped hands, and she looked over at my dish, and she said:

It looks so nice that I will not ask for any.

Now, when I heard that, I did smile. For I thought it the very prettiest way of asking for a thing I had ever heard.

And I thought of the people whose only way of asking God for things is to tease him, and say, Give me this, and be quick about it for Christ's sake.

For I wonder how folk dare to say for Christ's sake when they are asking something for their own sake, and whether it doth not sound unto the angels like swearing.

For of all the sins which good Christian men and women commit, it seemeth to me that among the gravest may be the undisguised selfishness of their prayers.

And I wondered how to teach Christian men and women to ask for things as prettily as the daughter of the daughter of Keturah asked for the Strawberry Sundae.

For I might just mention in closing that she got all the Strawberry Sundae she desired when she asked for it in that way. ❧

The
Long Walk

The daughter of the daughter of Keturah hath a little
friend who cometh to see her, and playeth with her in the
yard, hard by the Window, where their voices may be heard
inside the House. And mostly they play very Happily; but
now and then for the sake of Variety they indulge in
Argument and Comparison like grown Folk. And it was
upon a day that they got thus into a Friendly Scrap, the first
part of which I heard not. But the Argument had reached a
stage where the daughter of the daughter of Keturah was
advancing and backing the other little damsel off the Map,
and the other little girl could only answer, I did not, or You
can not, or It is not.

And the daughter of the daughter of Keturah said,
I can walk Fifty-nine miles.

And the other little girl said, you can not.

And the daughter of the daughter of Keturah said, I
can take my Grandpa's hand and keep up with him, and he
can walk Fifty-nine miles, and I can walk Fifty-nine miles
with him if I hold his hand.

And the other little damsel said, You can not.

Then did the daughter of the daughter of Keturah tell
unto the other little girl how great and good a Grandpa she

had. And I am too modest a man to write down what she said; but if George Washington and Solomon and a few others were to live in one, peradventure he might be a Second-cousin or a Remote Acquaintance of a man such as the daughter of the daughter of Keturah described.

And the other little girl could only change the subject, and say,

I can kick your whole house down and all your trees.

And the daughter of the daughter of Keturah, knowing that she had won out, said sweetly,

Go ahead.

Now there is no man who knoweth so well as I how far from right is the estimate of the little maiden concerning the goodness and the greatness of her Grandpa. Nevertheless it pleased me more than any man can understand who is not a Grandpa; for unto none others hath the Lord given wisdom to know of such matters. And the next time a man goeth by and bloweth a small whistle, she shall have a Red Balloon.

For apart from her beautiful delusion concerning the poor man concerning whom I pray my God that she may be never undeceived, the little maiden is not wholly wrong. For when she holdeth my hand she can do things which otherwise she could not do.

And I prayed unto my God a prayer, and I said,

O my God, Thou hast permitted us through the gift of little lives such as these to discern spiritual truths which thou hast hid from the wise and prudent and revealed unto babes, that so we might enter into the Kingdom of Heaven as little children. Grant unto me this, O my Father, that I shall hold so fast to Thine Hand that the journey that would otherwise be impossible shall be possible for me, and the task that would have been too great may be accomplished through thy strength. For I can do all things through Him that strengtheneth me and if I hold His Hand I can run and not be weary, and walk and not faint. ❧

The
Lost Tooth

The daughter of the daughter of Keturah came unto our habitation, and she sought the Cookie Box of Keturah. And thus did Keturah's own children in their day. And thus have I done often. Save that I never eat one Cookie. I can eat none and I can eat four or five, but I cannot eat one of the Cookies of Keturah and stop. And the little maiden ate of the Cookies of Keturah. And I think that there will always be Cookies in her Cookie Box.

Now as the damsel ate, she cried out in terror.

And I wondered what had happened unto her, for that is not the way the Cookies of Keturah affect people.

And she cried not in pain, but in terror. And she said, Oh, Grandpa, my tooth has come out!

And she held up a tiny front tooth in her little hand.

Now the loss of a Tooth is a matter of some importance to me; for I fear lest the time come when the grinders cease because they are few. But I knew that for her it was not a serious matter.

And I comforted her, and I said, Fear not. It is of no consequence.

And she said, Oh, Grandpa, canst thou put it back?

And I told her that I could not, and that I would not if I could.

And she understood it not, but she was comforted when she saw that I did not share her fear.

And I said, Have no fear, my little girl. The teeth that God gave thee when teeth first came unto thee, were baby teeth, and they will leave thee one by one, and fall out. Trouble not thyself, for there shall grow others in their place that will be stronger and better and last longer.

And she was comforted.

Then I considered the losses of life, and the pain and the fear of them, and how they are even as the fear that was in the heart of the little maiden when she lost the Tooth. Yea, I went where people suffered by reason of losses which I could not explain so easily, and my words of comfort had behind them no knowledge of what blessing God should provide instead of the thing that had been taken away.

But I remembered that it is written in the Word of God how God hath provided Some Better Thing.

And I took the little pearly tooth from the hand of the little maiden, and she sat upon my knee and ate the residue of her Cookie, and I stroked her Golden Hair, and I prayed unto God for all those who have losses in life and who know not how God shall provide any better thing in place of them.

For their sorrow is like unto the sorrow of the daughter of the daughter of Keturah, and there are times when my wisdom stoppeth short of their need. 🙵

The
Transformed Tooth

The daughter of the daughter of Keturah lost a Tooth. And she carried it about in her hand, and she showed it with great Pride. And she said, Behold the Tooth which I had, and which came out this morning. And behold, here is the place where it grew, and another shall grow in its place; for thus hath my Grandpa told me.

Now she showed it unto one who said unto her,

Wrap thou the Tooth in Paper, and put it under thy Pillow tonight, and it will turn into a Dollar.

And she came home and told her mother. And she said, Here is a piece of Paper, and I will wrap my Tooth in it; and in the morning the Tooth will be gone, and in its place will there be a Dollar.

And her mother could not permit that the little maiden should break her heart or suffer disappointment; therefore did she not forbid it.

And after the little maiden was asleep, then her mother considered what was best to be done.

And in the morning the little damsel awoke, and she felt under her Pillow, and behold, there was no tooth there, but a Dollar.

And she ran down the stairs, and she cried with a loud

voice, saying, Behold, mother, what hath happened; for my Tooth hath turned into a Dollar.

And she took the money to the Bank and added to her Savings Account.

And the little damsel considered, and she asked of her mother and inquired, saying, How many teeth have I?

And her mother said, Thou hast Twenty and Four.

And she asked, Will they all come out?

And her mother answered, Yea, and more will grow in their place.

Then began the little maiden to consider how that she could Support the Family with the Unearned Increment from her Teeth. For she said, Mother, I have twenty and four teeth, and every one of them shall turn into a Dollar. Consider how Rich we shall be.

And her mother told it unto me.

And she asked, Ought I to have told her that the Tooth turneth not into a Dollar, and that her friend lied unto her? For behold, these are the days of the High Cost of Living; and if I am in for twenty and four dollars to provide the means for this transformation, that is a little more money than I contemplated.

And I said, Trouble not thyself. The little maiden will face quite soon enough the stern, hard facts of life. Deprive her not of her little happy illusions, nor seek to fetter too soon with the shackles of Grim Reality the precious gift of the Imagination. For this is the gift of God, and we of this age do too much clip its wings. Behold, here is a Dollar into which the next Tooth may be transformed, and when thou seest another Tooth working loose, come again to thy father.

For the little maiden hath learned a very precious thing, which is to make an asset of one's losses, and to transform the vacant interstices of life into opportunities of larger promise. I would she could teach unto all of God's creatures that if they will lay their losses under their pillow, and go to sleep with faith in God, the night worketh a wonderful transformation, and joy cometh in the morning. For this is my hope, even when I lay away not a Tooth only but the body of which the Tooth is a part, that the day shall dawn and the shadows flee away. For His is the image and superscription upon the coinage of that into which life's losses are convertible in the morning of the new day.

And I shall be satisfied when I awake with His likeness. ❧

The Cocoanut Cakes

I was not always aged, but was once young. And I sojourned in a School of the Prophets. And on the day before the Sabbath I rode every week Nineteen Miles that on the Sabbath Day I might speak the word of God to the people in a Little White Church with a Tall Steeple. And on the day after the Sabbath I rode back again. And there were times when the Roads were bad, so that for every foot that my horse went forward, he sank in the mud unto the depth of an half of a foot; so I went down through Nine Miles and the half of a Mile of mud before I got there. But when I arrived then did the good people welcome me into warm homes and clean beds and set before me hot suppers.

For I boarded around among them.

And at the first place where I abode for a Sabbath, the good woman set before me Cocoanut Cake. And I ate plentifully thereof.

Now the women of the other homes inquired of her, saying, How didst thou like the Young Minister? And is he hard to entertain? And doth he cause thee much trouble? And is he fussy? And what doth he like to eat?

And she said, He is not fussy, and he said unto me that Cocoanut Cake is his Favorite Cake.

THE COCOANUT CAKES

Now all the women told all the other women, saying The Young Minister loveth Cocoanut Cake.

And they all knew how to make Cocoanut Cake, and they all made it. And wherever I went, there did they set before me Cocoanut Cake.

Now thou wilt surely think within thine heart that I got so much Cocoanut Cake that I abhorred it, and that I have never liked it since. But thou hast another Think coming. For thou knowest not what sort of Cocoanut Cake the women of that Parish make. Yea, for three years did I eat it with scarce ever a break in the record, save that there also they make Cake with Maple Sugar Frosting. And he that hath eaten that kind of Cake knoweth that that is about the best ever.

For there be some things of which no one can ever have too much. And when mine heart goeth back across the years, then do I remember the long rides, and the times that I drave up in the dark and the cold, and how they stabled mine horse knee-deep in clean straw, and put a sack of oats under the buggy-seat when I departed, and maybe also a Bushel of Potatoes or a Sack of Apples or a Can of Maple Syrup. And I know that I shall never have too much of any of the good things which they bestowed upon me, nor of the love that was in them all.

And now and then as the years go by, and one and another of those I loved is called home, then do they send for me to come and say a word of love before the dust returneth unto dust. And ever there is some good woman who hath a table set for me in her home; and there do I always find Cocoanut Cake.

And whenever I eat of Cocoanut Cake that is Unusually Nice, then do I remember the friends of my early Ministry as a Messenger of God, and I love them yet.

The Woodpecker

Now, on a morning I entered my Study, and I sat me down to read a book by a Learned Man on The Uniformity of Nature. And I thought much about the Reasons Why the Heat that Burneth a person on one day doth not Freeze him on the next, and why the Sun which Riseth in the East a part of the Time doth not Rise in the West the Remainder of the Time, and why the Law of Gravitation which sometimes pulleth the Apple Down doth not sometimes Hurl it Up.

And These Studies proved a Weariness to the Flesh, so that I opened my window for Fresh Air. And immediately there flew in a Woodpecker. And no sooner was he in than he wished to be out. And he circled Twice or Thrice about my Ceiling, and then flew swiftly toward another Window which was not open, and Struck it with all his Force, so that he Fell to the floor and lay there as if he were Dead. And I Rose, and Stood, and looked down at him. And I touched him not, but it was revealed to me that in his Aching Red Head he was thinking thoughts like these:

Behold, hitherto have I flown wherever there was Transparent Space, and have Struck Nothing. But I have been Knocked Down and well-nigh Killed while flying through Space in which I could see plainly. Yea, and beyond were Trees, and the Free Air of Spring. Never again shall I trust in the Uniformity of Nature; and the ways of the Lord are not equal.

Then I left him, and I opened my windows from the top downward and he rose and flew straight at one of them, and was gone.

And I, who am but very little wiser than he, meditated concerning those I have known who suddenly come Up Against a new experience which they are unable to Catalogue among their Theories of life, where something which they see not riseth up before them and layeth them low, so that they cry out in their anguish that the Lord hath forgotten to be Gracious, and that His Mercy is clean gone forever. For I have heard them think aloud even as I heard the woodpecker with the Aching Red Head.

Now the Uniformity of Nature is the Veracity of God. Yet hath God ways that are not as the ways of His creatures. So I besought my God that he would give me Grace to Trust Him when I fly through what seemeth Clear Space and come Up against Something. ⚓

Of Knowing
Too Little
and Too Much

There came to the City wherein I dwell a man who delivered a Lecture, and I and Keturah we went. And the subject whereof he spake was one about which he knew very little. But he spread that little over the surface of an Interesting Talk, and the people enjoyed it and so did we. Yea, and we were profited thereby, although the Lecturer knew little more than he told us.

And there came another man who spake on the same subject, and we went to hear him. And he was a man of Great Erudition. And I said, Now shall we hear something Worth While.

But he began by telling us the History of the Subject and the Various Attempts to Elucidate it. And then he spake of the Various Theories that had been Suggested concerning it, and the books that had been written in Divers Tongues with regard to it. And he said that a certain opinion had been held by scholars, but was now no longer highly regarded, but that the opinion that was to take its place was in dispute. And he suggested Various Aspects of the theme which he said he could not Discuss because it would require a Volume on any one of them.

And about that time it was time to stop, and he stopped.

And as we journeyed toward our home, Keturah said, He certainly is a man of large knowledge.

And I answered, Yea, and for the purposes of that audience it were better if he had known the tenth part of what he knoweth. For the first man carried all his goods in his show-window, and this man blocked the sidewalk with dray-loads of unopened cases and bales of unassimilable and useless wisdom.

And Keturah said, I have heard that a Little Knowledge is a Dangerous thing.

And I said, Believe it not. A little knowledge is good for seed, but there is such a thing as that a person getteth drowned in his own knowledge. For the first man knew little, but used that little effectively, and the second man knew much, and it was useless.

And I said unto Keturah, Like unto a Spider that is entangled in its own web, so is the person of much knowledge who is unable to employ it. Better is it to know little and be able to use it wisely, than to know much and to get lost in the swamp of it.

And Keturah said, Nevertheless, I think that knowledge is good, and much knowledge is better than little.

And I said, All human knowledge is small, and the difference between the one who knoweth much and the one who knoweth little is too small to waste much time in futile distinctions. For in the sight of God the wisdom of both is foolishness. But the value of knowledge is in the use of it.

And Keturah inquired of me, saying, Art thou a man of much knowledge or of little?

And I answered, If so be that I am able to use my knowledge and get away with it, what doth it matter if it be little or large? Behold, though I be ignorant, yet have I no trouble in finding people yet more ignorant, and if the stream wherein they swim is over their head, what doth it matter if it be an inch or ten thousand cubits?

And Keturah said, I do verily believe that among the ignorant men of earth there be some who are more ignorant than thee; and if any of them do think thee wise, I shall not tell them that it is not so. ࿇

Concerning
Rest

There was a day when I was weary. For my days had been full of cares, and my nights had been broken. And I spake unto Keturah, saying,

I would fain Lay me down upon my Couch and rest. Trouble me not for the Space of One Hour.

So I laid me down.

And I heard the Patter of Little Feet, and there were Little Hands pushing at my door. And there came unto me the daughter of the daughter of Keturah.

And she said, Grandpa, I want to lie down with you.

And I said, Come, and we will rest together. Close thine eyes Tightly and be Very Still. So shall we rest both of us.

And the way she rested was this. She crept under the Blanket that covered me, so that her head and all the rest of her were Covered, and she said, Grandpa, you have losed your little girl.

Then did I seek my little girl whom I had losed, and I said, Where is my little girl? Where is my little girl? And I felt all over the Blanket, and I found her not.

Then did she cry, Here I am.

And she threw off the Blanket, and laughed.

And she hid from me the Second Time, and the Third Time, and Many Times beside. And every time I found her again, hiding under the Blanket.

And when this had wearied her, she Sat Astride me, so that One Foot was on the Right Side and one was on the Left, and she held me by the thumbs, and her little hands could not quite reach around my two thumbs. And she rocked back so that her head touched the couch between my knees, and she sat up with a Bump upon my Stomach. And she rode me to Banbury Cross and to many other places.

And she said, You are having a good time with me, aren't you, Grandpa?

And I told her that it was true.

Now at the end of One Hour, I came forth leading the little damsel by the hand, and Keturah said, Thou art rested. I behold that thy weariness is gone.

And it was even so. For the joy of playing with the little damsel had driven away my care, and I was rested.

Now I thought of this, and I remembered that my Lord had said, Come unto me, ye weary and heavy-laden, and I will give you rest. And I remembered that He said that in resting I should bear a yoke and find it easy, and carry a burden and find it light. And, behold, I knew what He meant. ❧

Failure
and Success

Keturah made a Cake. And the manner of making it was this. She baked it in Three Sections, and when they came from the Oven, she laid them one upon another so that the Cake was Three Stories in Height. And between the layers she placed Frosting, yea, and more Frosting upon the top thereof. And into the Frosting did she put handfuls of meat out of the Cocoanut. For there be many kinds of cake that I like, even every kind that Keturah doth make, but the best of all is the kind that is made with Cocoanut.

And when she served the Cake, she said, Alas, it is a Failure.

And I said, Wherefore should it be a Failure?

And she answered, The Telephone did ring just when the Frosting should have been attended to, and it hath not sufficiently hardened. Yea, it is Sticky, and a Failure.

And when I beheld it, lo, very much of the Frosting had run down the sides of the Cake. Nevertheless, there was much of it still upon the top, and between the layers, and the Cocoanut was all to the Good.

And I said, Since it is a Failure, it were well to eat more of it, and put the Poor Thing out of Sight.

And Keturah said, Thou hast well said. Eat thou another slice, and yet another.

And I did as I was bidden. And albeit the Cake was a trifle Sticky, there was nothing else that was not one hundred per cent to the good.

Therefore, when she maketh something that is Unusually Good, I say unto her, Is not this a Failure? For I desire another piece.

And I would that we might somehow readjust life that all life's Failures might somehow make for success. Yea, I remember that my God hath promised that in some way that I know not the wrath of man shall praise him.

For if this world, which is a cake not turned, can scrape some of the char from its overdone side, and bake the side that is dough so that it can be eaten, then shall I rejoice. For I would believe that this world is a success, and by faith I so accept it.

The
Pins

Now it was the Sabbath Day, and I rose and washed myself and attired myself in Clean Raiment, and went to the House of God. And it came to pass that I sought in the Middle Drawer and I found therein a Clean Shirt which had been sent home from the Laundry. And the bosom thereof shone like polished Alabaster; and the Starch therein was so stiff that one might scarcely open the Buttonholes without a Screwdriver.

And before I could put it on I pulled out Sundry Pins which the Laundry had placed therein, and there were many Pins in the Shirt.

And After I had pulled out Pins enough to hold the Solar System in place, I put on the Shirt.

But I had overlooked One Pin.

And I went to the Synagogue, and I sat down; and I found that there remained a Pin in the Garment from which I had withdrawn so many Pins.

And I changed my Position so that the Pin no longer hurt me, and I forgot about it for a season. But when we had risen up to Praise the Lord in Song, and had sat down again, behold the Pin hurt me again, and in quite another portion of mine Anatomy. And later I found it still Elsewhere.

And when I had returned to my house I removed my Garments and I sought for the Pin and found it, and removed it; and it hurt me no more.

And I said to my soul,

Take not overmuch Comfort in the faults thou hast removed; neither be thou self-righteous. Behold, while one Pin remaineth in thy Shirt, did it not hurt thee in Twenty Places? Even so is one fault which thou removest not. Therefore let no one cherish pride until he be perfect; and if the time come when he count himself perfect, lo this belief is the one remaining Pin. Yea, and it is long like a Hatpin, and jabbeth both himself and others. Wherefore beware of self-righteousness; and see thou forget not to remove the Pins that remain. ॐ

The New Recipe

There was a morning when I rose from my bed, and looked at the sunrise, and thanked God that I was alive, even as I do each day. And I descended and came down, and ate my breakfast. And behold upon the table there were Doughnuts. Now if there be Doughnuts, I eat of them, but they minish not in any wise the other things that I eat, for I eat of them last.

And I said unto Keturah, Hast thou bought Sinkers from the Market? For I had not smelled the cooking of them.

And she said, I have not, for I value my peace of mind. I made these. Yea, and I made them by a New Recipe.

And I said, Wherefore wilt thou try New Recipes when already thy Doughnuts are perfect?

And she said, It is not thus that thou dost preach, for thou dost ever exhort folk to do better and better.

And I said, Thine aspiration to have things better and better is thine only fault. Thou dost even try to have it so with thy Husband.

And she said, Yea, and thus far I have done very well in the matter of his improvement.

So I ate of the Doughnuts, and I said, Behold, these are just like all of thy Doughnuts.

And she said, I am glad that thou dost think so. For they are so made that they absorb less Fat; therefore are they the more Wholesome.

And I said, Go not too far with me in that Wholesome stunt; I do not want things too Wholesome; I can digest anything save it be Health Foods.

And she said, When I try a New Recipe, thus do I try it. I consider all the things that I have been wont to use that I know are good, and if I find in the New Recipe some other good thing, that also do I put in.

And I said, Keturah, thou hast the finest idea of Progress to be found in any cook on earth. For thou goest ahead, but thou playest not far from thy Base.

And I said, If all reformers would learn of thee, then would the Millennium come sooner.

And she said, I am glad that thou dost like the new Doughnuts.

And I verily did like them. For they had one ingredient that changest not, and that is Keturah. ❧

Rising Above
the Clouds

I rode upon a Railway Train; and we were in the Rocky Mountains. And we awoke in the morning, and the Train was climbing, with two Engines pulling us, and one pushing behind. And we were nigh unto Twelve Furlongs above the Sea.

And it came to pass as we ascended, that there were clouds below us, and Clouds upon the sides of Mountains, but there were no Clouds above us, but the clear shining of the Morning Sun.

And there came unto me a small Girl and her younger Brother, who were riding upon the Train, and we talked about the Clouds. For so did John Ruskin, and Aristophanes, and the little lad was very happy, and he said,

I have never been above the Clouds before.

And his sister was Worldly-wise. And she said, A Cloud ain't nothing but just fog.

And he said, Nay, but this is more. And behold now, how then is a Cloud just under us, and we ride upon the top of it?

And she said, We are on the Rails, just as we always have been; and there can't nobody ride on a cloud.

And the boy said, Jesus can ride upon a Cloud; for I saw a Picture of Him.

And the little girl said, Yes, but that ain't us.

Now the little girl may have been right; but I thought within myself that this world hath too many people who look out on Life through her windows. For they see no sunlit Clouds, but only Fog; and they have little faith in rising above Clouds, but have confidence only in the Rails.

And I do not despise Rails, nor advise people to discard them and ride upon Clouds. Nevertheless, I have seen people rise above Clouds, and live in the sunlight of God. And I have known others who, whenever it is said unto them, Thus have others done, or thus did the good Lord Jesus, make reply, Yes, but that ain't us.

And if it is spoken concerning the House of God, Thus did the Synagogue in Jonesville, and thus was it done by the Church in Smithville, they answer, Yes, but that ain't us.

And if it be said, Thou shouldest be a better person; for others have risen above thy Clouds and thine Infirmities, they say, Yes, but that ain't us.

And when it is said, Thus hath the grace of God abounded in other lives, they say, Yes, but that ain't us.

But if it ain't, why ain't it?

For this cause did God dwell in human flesh that we should never count any good thing impossible through the dear Lord Jesus.

For he is our peace, who hath broken down all middle walks, that we should no longer say, But that ain't us.

Crumbs
and Bubbles

Now I was meditating on the things that seem to be Trivial and how when they are many, they become an Heap so that they Block the Amenities of Life.

And I listened and I heard the Patter of Little Feet, and I stopped my work, and the daughter of the daughter of Keturah ran into mine arms, and pulled my Beard, and kissed me upon both of my cheeks and once beside, and she said:

Grandpa, this day is my Birthday, and behold there hath been given unto me a Doll, and a Cake with Candles thereupon.

And I said unto her, It was a glad day when God sent thy Mother unto us, and another glad day when He did send thee; and behold the years have gone so fast that when I hold thee in mine arms, I know not if it be thee or thy mother.

And she said, Grandpa, Behold it Snoweth. Take me out that I may behold the Snow.

So I took her out, wrapped in her Double Garments, and she rejoiced in the Snow. And she beheld how it came down in her face in what she called Little Bubbles, for they melted straightway, and how it fell upon my coat in what she called Little Crumbs.

For it is on this manner that she fitteth the words that she knoweth to her New Experiences, and oft do I marvel at the way in which she findeth a word for the thing she hath not known. And I considered her use of the words Bubbles and Crumbs of Snow. And we went within the house, and watched through the window, and we saw the Snow strike the window in Bubbles, and fall outside in Crumbs. And the Crumbs and the Bubbles were both Very Little Things.

Now when the morning was come, Behold the Snow was piled at my door in a Great Drift. And I listened, and behold there were no Trains, and I waited, and behold there were no Mails. And certain of my neighbors had no Coal and could not get it.

And I considered, and said, Behold the Crumbs of Snow and the Bubbles of Snow that fell in the face of the Little Maiden, and on the Overcoat of her Grandfather. How small were they one by one, and behold they Stop the Trains.

And I considered that it is even so with many things in life that are small in themselves, but when multiplied they become Habits that people cannot break, or Grievances that rend Friendships Asunder, even as Great Drifts are made of Bubbles and Crumbs of Snow. ❧

The Dog
and the Limited

Now I rode on a Fast Express Train called the Limited. And we went through a Country where there were Many Farms. And the Train went like the Driving of Jehu.

And there was a Farmhouse that stood near unto the track but back, as it were, about the space of a Furlong. And in the Farmhouse dwelt a Farmer. And the Farmer had a Dog. And when the Train drew Nigh, the Dog started from the Farmhouse toward the Train. And he Barked Furiously, and he Ran Swiftly. And I marveled that he could run so Swiftly, and that at the same time he could Bark so Furiously. But with all his barking he could not make so much Noise as the Train, neither with all his Running could he overtake it.

And the path that he made in his Running was a Great Parabolic Curve. For he started before the Train entered the Farm, running toward the Train, and going East, for the Train was toward the West. But as the Train ran on and stopped not, the Dog ran South, and when the Train was going By and not even Hesitating, he Curved so that he ran Southwest and then West. And at the west side of the Farm he fell into a Ditch, and rolled over and over and got up, and shook himself, and stood for a moment and cursed the Train, and then Returned Home.

And the Train went on.

And a month thereafter I rode on the same Train, and behold, the Same Dog did all the Things that he had done before.

And three months thereafter I rode again on the Same Train, and the Same Fool Dog was still Getting Experience in the Same Manner, but Learning Nothing Therefrom.

And I saw that he was even like unto some of us, who might be Brayed in a Mortar with a Pestle, yet would not our Folly depart.

For even as that Dog watcheth daily for that Train, rising every morning and listening for it, and chasing it through the Farm, and Tumbling in the Ditch on the West Line of the Farm, so there are those who Chase their Follies Continually, and learn Nothing from their Tumbles.

And what would the Dog have Done with the Train if he had Caught it? ❧

The Bath Tub
at the Inn

Now it came to pass as I journeyed that I lighted on a certain place where there was an Inn, and I entered and Lodged there. And in the Inn was a Bath Tub, and but one; and every Saturday night each Guest did bathe himself or herself therein. And I beheld them as they Furtively Hastened through the halls, clad in Bathrobes or in something less, and they were not Naked, yet did they hasten as if ashamed.

And in time it came about that I Obtained Entrance into the Bath Room, just as Another Man was Leaving it. And he wore a Ragged Bathrobe, and a Smile that said, Behold, I am clean.

And I entered, and the Water still was Running from the Tub, and Gurgling as it ran.

And I looked within the Tub, and behold, there was on the inside of it a Ridge, which marked the Level of the Water at the time the last Occupant had been within. And I liked it not.

Then I communed with my soul, and my soul said to me, Doest thou well to be Wroth with the man who last Bathed? Behold the Ridge around the tub. Is it not evidence that he hath had a bath? Yea, doth it not show that he

Needed one? Yea, furthermore, doth it not prove that the bath hath Wrought Well for him, and that by the Measure of whatever thou seest on the Sides of the tub, and what hath run down the pipe, the man is Cleaner than when he entered? Lovest thou not truth, and the evidence thereof? And is not Cleanliness a Virtue wherein thou shouldst Rejoice?

And I said, Yea, I rejoice in the Truth, but the Evidence giveth me no Pleasure; and I Love Virtue, and Cleanliness is a virtue, yet I would that he had given me other proof of his Cleanliness, or given me none at all.

Then I considered within myself, and I meditated thus. Behold, there are many who practice their virtues in such form that they make virtue unlovely. Yea, there be those who serve the Lord as if the devil were in them. &

The Moth in the Church Carpet

There was a Moth that had his home in the Sanctuary, and he lived long and was happy. For the place of his Habitation was between Two Tacks, in the edge of the Carpet, in an obscure little Angle where the stair ascendeth unto the Pulpit. And it would have been difficult to select a Finer Place of abode for a Moth of Sedentary Habits. And he never, never wandered from his own fireside, but whitened the Corner Where He was. That is to say, he wandered not until the time when this Chapter in his History Beginneth, and this Chapter is not a long one, and there will not be any Chapters after this. For that Moth is there no longer, and the place that knew him knoweth him no more.

Now this Moth was Serenely Happy; for the carpet was Fuzzy, and it was the Very Best Food a Moth could desire, and the Brushes of the Janitor came not nigh him.

And the Moth listened unto the Organ, and he thought the Musick was for his Edification, and he heard the Sermons and the Prayers, and so far as he knew they were addressed to him.

And he lifted up his eyes, and behold, there were Yards and Yards of Carpet, stretching down Long Aisles through the length of the Nave, and he looked unto the right hand and the left, and there was Carpet unto the uttermost borders of the Transepts. And the lines had fallen unto him in pleasant places, and he had a goodly heritage.

But he waxed fat, and grew Conceited. And he said, Go to, now; I will explore mine Heritage; for, behold, all this is mine, and for me it hath been created.

And he crept out of his Corner, and started on a journey down the Center Aisle.

And when he had gotten out about an Inch and the half of an Inch, behold, the Janitor came along with a Vacuum Cleaner, and just what happened unto the Moth, he hath not yet clearly defined in his own mind. For he was sucked up with a strong wind, and pulled down an hollow rod, and blown down a rubber tube that led to an Iron Pipe into a Vat in the Basement, and buried deep in Dust. And while he meditated, the Janitor came, and opened the Vat, and thrust in a Shovel, and scooped up the Dust and shoveled it into the Blazing Fiery Furnace, and the moth was in the Dust when this occurred. And the History of that Moth from that time on containeth nothing of importance. But there seldom hath been a Moth whose Future Prospects were more encouraging than that one, if he had not gotten a Swelled Head, and thought that he was Boss of the Whole Establishment.

Now the person who thinketh that the Universe was made for his own convenience would better stay in his own little corner of it; for if he getteth out where Important Things Occur, something is likely to happen either unto him or his Theory. 🙢

Things
Sweet

There was a day when Keturah called unto me to come to Lunch. And I came in and sat down over against her.

And she said, Give thou thanks unto God.

And I inquired of her, saying, What for?

And she asked of me, saying, Hast thou no faith?

And I said, I have faith, and that is very nearly all. For I see nothing that I might eat, save thee and a pound of Honey.

And she said, I should think that either one of us might justify thee in giving thanks.

And I said, It is even so, and I will do it. For thou and the pound of Honey are about the Same Size and there are other qualities possessed in Common by the two of you.

And Keturah said, Be brief with thy nonsense, and ask God's blessing on the food. For though it be an act of faith, yet shall thy faith bear fruit if thou delay not until the residue of the luncheon burn.

So we bowed our heads, and we gave thanks unto God for each other, and for our Home, and for our Children and for our Friends, and for the Food that I had faith to believe was coming.

Then went Keturah to the Kitchen, and she returned with a Wondrous Corn Cake.

Now the color of it was the color of Pure Gold refined in the fire. And the Odour of it was a Sweet Smell. And the appearance thereof was enough to make the mouth of a Dyspeptick water.

And she cut the Golden Corn Cake, and gave unto me a Great Square of it, an Acre or less in Area. And I cut it in twain with a Knife, and laid the two halves upon my Plate, and spread it over with Butter, and then I laid honey upon the top.

And when I had eaten it all, then did I pass back my plate, and Keturah gave unto me another Acre or less. And that also did I eat.

Now there was a time in our early married life when Keturah was wont to say, Take heed that thou eat not too much of food such as this. But she saith that no longer.

And I ate, until I desired no more.

And I said, Keturah, there is less of the Honey, but thou art the same. And I said something further to her about the Honey and Herself, but that is not for Publication. Only this I thought, how good it is for a man to have Food and plenty of it, and to have it rich and sweet and wholesome, and to have an Home that is sweet and companionable, and to have an Appetite and a Job.

Now I have read that George Washington ate plentifully of Corn Cake and Honey; and I marvel not that he was great.

Beloved, see to it that thou keep thy tastes Simple and Normal, and that thou love thine own Home. For the age in which we live hath great need of these very elementary lessons in the science of Right Living. 🙠

How I
Obtained
the Philosopher's
Stone

Now in the days of my youth there was a Wise Man, who had lived to a Great Age; and he had a Stone called the Philosopher's Stone, wherein he looked and Saw Strange Things, and Understood Great Mysteries. And all of his friends Wondered what he would do with the Stone when he Died. And it came to pass that he sent out Messengers to all the Prophets and Sages and Soothsayers, and said unto them:

Behold, I go the way of all flesh, and before I go I shall give this Stone to the one who is to Follow after me. Come ye, then, all who are wise, and let me discover which of you is Worthy, that he may Inherit this Stone.

And most of those who were Reputed Wise began to make Excuse, for they Feared to Come, lest he should Lay Bare their Folly; and they sent him Messages saying that they had Previous Engagements, but hoped that he would send them the Stone by Parcels Post, and they would pay the Freight.

But there were seven men who went, from seven cities;

and they came before him. And he sat in his Chair, and he had a long white beard, and he commanded the seven wise men to stand before him.

And thus he spake to them —

This Stone, which was brought to earth by a Meteor, and found by a man who was a Seventh Son of a Seventh Son, I shall give to the man among you who Returneth the Right Answer to the Question which I shall ask. Are you ready for the Question?

And certain of the Wise Men Answered and said to him, We are ready. Ask us whatsoever Question thou wilt. Ask it in the Firmament or in the Earth; in the Land or in the Sea; in Things Movable or Things Immovable; lo, we are Ready.

Then, said he, I will ask you this Question: What is the Best Way for a Man to help a Woman over a Fence?

And they were all Dumb for a season, for truly he had put them up against a Hard One.

Then answered the first of the Wise Men, and said, He should stand with her upon the nearer side, and with his right hand under her left elbow should gently lift her the while she climbeth.

And the second answered, and said, He should kneel upon one knee, and let her step in his hand, as if she were to mount an Horse.

And the third said, He should himself climb over first, and offer her his hand, while she Gracefully Steppeth down on the Farther Side.

And the fourth said, He should indeed climb over first, and she should climb to the Top, and when she Sitteth There upon the Top of the Fence, he should put up both hands, not permitting her to climb down, but should cause her to Leap Boldly and Gracefully into his Arms.

And the fifth said, He should assail the Fence, and carry it away as Samson did the Gates of Gaza, so should he make an highway for her to pass through.

And the sixth said, The way for a Man to help a Woman over a Fence is to Walk with her till they find a Gate, and open the Gate and walk through with her; and the Lovelier the Lady, the farther should it be to the Gate.

Now when they had all spoken, they waited for the Ancient Man to award the Stone. And he said, Have ye all spoken?

And they answered and said, We have spoken.

And they had forgotten me, for I was the youngest of them all. But the Ancient Man had seen me. And he beckoned with the hand, and I drew near and he said to me:

Young man, what sayest thou? With Which of these Six Men dost thou Agree?

And I answered, With none of them.

Then said he, Speak thou, and tell us what is the Best Way for a Man to help a Woman over a Fence?

And I answered and said, The Best Way for a Man to help a Woman over a Fence is for him to cross over, and go on a little space about his Business, yet not too far; and let her Climb over Any Old Way that Pleaseth her.

Then were they all silent.

And he gave the Stone to me. ❧

The Musickal
Education

Once upon a time there was a man who had a daughter. And he loved Musick. And as the damsel grew, she sang; and the singing gladdened his heart and the heart of her mother. And they bought her a Piano, and hired a Teacher, who came to the house and gave her lessons at Fifty Cents an Hour. And the lesson was worth every cent of it. For the damsel soon could play Scales and Exercises, and between times would pick out Tunes with one finger, to the great joy of her father.

And when the time came that she could take the Hymn Book and sit down on Sunday afternoon, and play The Sweet Bye and Bye without very many Mistakes, her father wiped his eyes and thanked God for his daughter and for her Musickal Attainments. And there were evenings when the young folk gathered, and she seated herself at the Piano and played the Suwanee River and Seeing Nellie Home, and they all sang and were glad.

Now there came an evil day when one spake unto the father, saying, Thy daughter hath Musickal Ability. Now therefore, send her away that she may study Musick.

So they sent her away to a Conservatory; and they shut down the cover of the Piano. And on Sunday afternoon her father said, It is lonely, but when she returneth she will play to Beat the Band.

And it came to pass that at the end of certain days she returned with a Musickal Education. And I was Among Those Present on the evening when they gave a Welcome Home Party. And the father said, Tonight we shall have Musick.

But on that night none of the other girls dared play, for they had not been away to a Conservatory. And the daughter would not play, for her Sheet Musick had not arrived. Neither would she sing, for she said that she was Out of Practice, having recently studied only Theory and Composition and Fugue and Counterpoint.

And I said unto her, It is not an Excess of Musickal Culture that aileth thee, but the need of Chastisement. In the days when thou couldest barely play The Sweet Bye and Bye so that it might be told from Yankee Doodle thy Musickal Talent was good for something. Thou wert a joy unto thy father and a comfort to thy mother; and thou couldest add happiness to the life of thy friends. But now thou knowest just enough to be Useless.

And I asked, Knowest thou any of the sweet old Ballads, as The Last Rose of Summer, or Coming Through the Rye?

And she said, Yea; but they are very Old and Simple.

And I said, Go thou to the piano, and play and sing. Thou hast given this party a Frost, and chilled the heart of all present. Go thou back and warm them up with something that they love.

And she did as I told her. And the heart of all present was warmed. And certain of the other girls played.

And as the hour waxed late, some of the young folk said, Let us sing some of Those Good Old Timers that we used to like. And she played for them.

So her Musickal Education did not quite spoil her after all. And when she hath a Musickal Education that is much better, she will know better the Worth of my lesson to her.

Concerning
Lemons

Now it came to pass that I journeyed to a far country called California. And there I found a friend, a citizen of that country, and he had an Automobile, and he took me on swift journeys to show me Orange Groves and Grape Fruit Orchards, and Vineyards, and many trees whereon grew Prunes.

And it came to pass that I heard often of a town called Corona, and always this was said of it:

Corona, Home of the Lemon.

Now on a day we passed through Corona, and the day was warm and dusty, and I spake to my friends:

Behold, this is Corona, the Home of the Lemon. Let us tarry, I pray thee, for of lemons are concocted a cunning drink that maketh glad the heart and doth not intoxicate.

So we rode through the street, and we came to a place where it was written:

Ice Cream, Soda Water, Sundaes and All Kinds of Soft Drinks.

And we alighted from the chariot, and went in, and behold, a man in a White Apron.

And I was about to speak to him, but my friend spake:

Be thou silent, and keep thy money in thine own pocket; I am paying for this.

And I kept silent willingly, for those are pleasant words to hear.

Then spake my friend to the man in the white apron: Hasten thee, lad, and prepare for us four good, ice-cold lemonades, and make them Good, and make them Speedily.

And the man in the White Apron heard him as one who understood not what he said.

Then spake my friend again:

This friend of mine is from Chicago, and these other friends are from Boston, and they think they know what good lemonade is; but I want them to have a drink of lemonade that is Lemonade. Hasten thee, and prepare it for them.

Then spake the man in the White Apron:

We have no Lemonade.

And the man of California grew red in the face, and he said: What? No lemonade in Corona, the home of the lemon?

And the man in the white apron answered, We have Soda Water, Root Beer, Ginger Ale, Ice Cream, but no lemonade.

Then spake my friend:

Hasten now to the grocery store, and buy a half-dozen good lemons, and quickly make us Lemonade.

And the man in the White Apron hastened, and returned, and said:

There isn't a lemon in town. They ship them all to Chicago and Boston.

And when I heard this I meditated, and I said:

I have suffered for lack of good Fish at the Seashore, and Fresh Eggs in the Country, when both were abundant in Town, and now I behold that the place to buy good Lemonade is where they do not raise Lemons.

And as I meditated, I remembered that in many other things the shoemaker's family goeth unshod.

Yea, this shall be to me as a Parable, lest having preached to others I should become a Castaway.

So I resolved that with all my exportation of the Gospel, I would keep some for Home Consumption. ⁊

The Boys
and the Snow-balls

There came a heavy fall of Snow, and the daughter of the daughter of Keturah ran in at noontide on her way home from school, and she was in Sorrow. And she wept, and said:

Those boys are just as mean as they can be. They threw snow-balls at me, and they got snow all over my Coat, and over my Cap, and in my Hair, and some of it went down my neck. And behold, I am all covered with snow, and the boys wait just around the Corner to throw more snow-balls at me.

And I took off her Coat, and shook it. And I took off her Cap, and placed it where it would dry. And I picked out snow from her Golden Hair and from her neck. And Keturah, she came also, and took the little girl to wash her face and wipe away the tears.

And I called up the daughter of Keturah and said, Thy daughter is here, and we desire that she shall lunch with us, and go back to school from here.

And the daughter of Keturah answered, It is well. So let her do.

Now Keturah had a Corking Good Lunch ready, and she set on another plate. And we all sat down, and gave God

77

thanks. And there was a bouquet upon the table, and Keturah turned it around so that the brightest flowers were toward the daughter of the daughter of Keturah. And Keturah said, The flowers desire to look across the table and to welcome our Little Girl.

And we had a Happy Luncheon together. And when it was over, I said, Now let me hear what Musick thou hast lately learned.

And she said, I still can play Holy Night, that I learned at Christmas; and I have a piece that is called The Butterfly, where one hand crosseth the other, and the Butterfly moveth up and down in pretty curves among the flowers which the other hand playeth.

And I said, Let us hear that.

And she said, I will do it. And, Grandpa, when I cross my hands, look thou, and behold how many Rings are on my fingers.

And I smiled at her little vanity concerning the Rings; neither did I reprove her: for she will outgrow all that if grown folk have sense enough to let her alone. And we had Fifteen Happy minutes at the Piano. And I remembered with what joy my father heard his Daughter and afterward his Granddaughter at the Piano, even as do I.

And the time came for the daughter of the daughter of Keturah to go back to school. And she said, What a happy time I have had, and this would not have come to me if those Naughty Boys had not thrown snow at me.

And I said, Thus doth the Good Lord God bring possibilities of good out of evil, and thus I hope it will be evermore.

And she said, I am glad I came. And I said, If I find those boys, I will thank them; but I will ask them not to do it Again. ❧

The Roll with the Strange Name

There came unto our home, our Little Grandson. And he besought his Grandmother, even Keturah, that she would give unto him a Roll. And she would have understood him plainly, but he said that he wanted a Pyonder Roll.

Now Keturah can make Pocket-Book Rolls, and Parker House Rolls, and Hot Biscuits, and if there be any kind of Rolls that are good, them also can she make. And when she serveth them with Golden Butter and Maple Syrup or Honey or Preserves, then would she cause the mouth of a Graven Image to water. But she did not know about any Pyonder Roll.

And the little lad said, I want the Roll that's called a Pyonder.

Then did a Great White Light begin to dawn upon the mind of Keturah, and she said, Tell me the rest of it, my dear.

And he said:

> *When the Trumpet of the Lord shall sound*
> *and Time shall be no more.*
> *And the Roll is called a Pyonder*
> *I'll be there.*

And she gave unto him a Roll, and he was there.

Now I bethought myself of the Strange Mental pictures which our Grown-up words bring unto the mind of children. And I considered that our Heavenly Father knoweth that our minds also are but the minds of Little Children, and all our Mental Pictures of Celestial Things are limited, and that much which we learn of Divine Truth is even as the Pyonder Roll.

And I am thankful that we have our Pyonder Rolls, even our Daily Bread, and that the way of essential righteousness is so plain that a little child may learn it. And it is my earnest hope that when the Roll is called Up Yonder, I'll be there. ❧

The Coffee
and the Doughnut

Keturah saved a Little Mess of Fat, and she made Doughnuts. And she gave them to me at Breakfast, and she said, Make much of them, for I know not when there will be more.

And I said, Unto him that hath for his Breakfast Coffee and Sinkers, sufficient unto the day is the evil thereof.

And as I was eating of the Doughnuts, Keturah said, All my Married Life have I endeavored to teach thee not to dip thy Doughnut in the Coffee. And thou doest it still, yea, and every one of thy sons doeth it also, as he hath learned it from thee. And the same is not permitted in Polite Society.

And I said, O thou fairest among women, and at times the most Unreasonable, why wilt thou mar a Sufficiently Satisfactory husband with overmuch of Perfectness?

I neither Drink nor Swear nor Smoke nor Chew, and Heaven is my home. I covet no other man's wife, though I wish that thou hadst been born Twins that I might marry thee both. Thou well mightest tremble at thy husband's approach to Faultlessness.

And Keturah answered, I have noticed no approach either to the Faultlessness or to the Trembling.

And I said, Then pay thou the more strict notice. For it

were not well for thee that thy husband should be an overgrown Fauntleroy. I know a Machinist who declareth that the Ideally Perfect Machine would not run, but must have a Saving Element of Ramshackleness; therefore must the Great Drive Wheels of the Locomotive be geared to an Eccentric. Behold now this Doughnut, that it doth attain to perfection by having in its center an Hole. Wherefore, be glad that thy husband hath the saving merit of a few small faults.

And she said, I took thee for better and for worse. If then, thou must dip thy Doughnut in thy Coffee, I will make the best of it. ❧

The Shoes
Under the Bed

Of Goodness there be many kinds. For a Shoe becometh good to wear when it becometh bad to look at. Wherefore do I complain when Keturah giveth away any of mine Old Shoes. And Keturah hath provided a place in the Closet, where they may stand in an Orderly Row; but it is my custom when I remove them at night to set them under the edge of the Bed. And at first there is one pair, and then there are other pairs, yea, and a pair of slippers also. And when I arise in the morning, I reach down with mine hand, and take up a Shoe, and if it be not the one that I would wear I set it back and find another.

Now with this System Keturah is not well pleased. Wherefore from time to time doth she gather them up, and set them in array in the Closet. And she saith unto me, Wherefore dost thou place thy shoes under the Bed, which is not Expedient neither Orderly, when thou might better place them in a Nice Straight Row in the Closet?

And I said, O thou fairest among women, were God to establish a school for Husbands, he would make thee Principal. Yea, and I am favored above all men in having become the First and only Graduate of that school, *Magna Cum Laude.*

And Keturah said, Thou hast learned many things, and in much thou hast done well. Yea, and I have yielded the Dipping of the Doughnut in the coffee; why wilt thou not pick up thy shoes?

And I said, If I must, then I needs must.

And I said, Thou hast an Hamper for soiled Clothing, and a Laundry Bag. I will put my Linen in the Laundry Bag, if thou wilt allow me a Little Latitude in the matter of the Shoes.

And Keturah said, For thee that will be doing very well.

And I answered and said, This will I do, even as I have promised, but O Keturah, I do not want to be Reformed any more than I am already Reformed.

And Keturah said, I verily believe that there are worse husbands, even than thou.

And then did she kiss me, which is a way that she hath.

Two Hands on One Boy

When I was a Little Boy I liked to have my Face and Hands Clean. But I had no love for the process by which they had to become clean. And many times I assumed that they were clean, when an Unbiased Observer might have held a Divergent Opinion. And my sons, when they were small, liked Cold Water about as well as their father did in his youth. But my Little Grandson is a Miracle of Cleanliness, and loveth to have his Face and Hands Washed. That is to say, he loveth our Little Joke.

And it came about on this wise. The little lad came to visit me and Keturah, and the time arrived for Lunch. And I said, Let us go and wash thy Hands. And he said, They need no washing.

Then said I, Let me wash One Hand and see how the other looketh beside it.

So I washed one of his hands.

Then I said, Place the Two Hands side by side, and let us see whether they belong both of them to the same boy.

And when we looked at them together, he agreed with me that those Two Hands could not belong to the Same Boy.

Then said I, Shall we wash the one that will make the Two Hands look alike?

And he said, Let us wash the Other Hand.

And when I had done it, he said, Now the Two Hands belong on the Same Boy. And he was right about it.

Then said I, Let us see if we can match the Two Clean Hands with a Clean Face.

And then I said, Thy face is Very Clean. Let us see if we can Comb thy Hair.

Now we have done this Many Times since that first day, and it hath become a Very Pleasant Joke with us, and a Merry Game.

And it is in this way we make progress in life. For the job of reforming any of us is too large for a Single Contract. But now and then we discover that we have improved a very little in one particular, and then we sometimes have grace enough to Wash the One Hand to make it match the virtue that we possess. And if the process continue Long Enough, there is hope that in time we may come so that the whole of us Shall Match ourselves at our best. ⅋

The Doughnuts

I sat me down at the Breakfast Table, and the smell of the Coffee was fragrant. And Keturah had cut a Grape Fruit so large that the half of it was as it were for a Bath Tub, and the juice thereof was delicious. And we also had Breakfast Food and Toast. And I looked about the Table, and I beheld some Doughnuts. And I shouted aloud for the joy thereof.

And Keturah said, I hope that thou wilt like them. I bought them at a Bakery Sale.

And I said, Keturah, thou hast betrayed the confidence of thine husband. I verily supposed that these Doughnuts were thine own.

And I took one of them, and brake it, and essayed to eat thereof.

And I said, Keturah, I am a more merciful man than to eat this Doughnut.

And she said, Toward whom art thou displaying mercy?

And I said, My heart goeth out unto the Little Birds, that flutter about in the cold, and have no nice juicy worms within reach. The north wind doth blow, and we shall have snow, and what will the birdies do then, poor things? They will see on the ground a doughnut so round, and they will be grateful to me, poor things.

And Keturah said, I am sorry that thou dost not like the Doughnuts that I provide.

And I said, I have no fault to find with the Doughnuts. I think that the Foundry where they were Cast had an unusually tough lot of Metal, but I am not criticizing the product. I care too much for the Birds to deprive them of such food.

So I went my way for that time, and I forgat about it. But when I returned home for Lunch, I smelled a Sweet Savour, and I cried aloud, Keturah, hast thou been making Doughnuts?

And she said, Taste these, and see if they be cast in the same Mould.

And I will not tell how many I consumed of them.

And I said, Behold, am not I a benefactor, and an Humane Man? For in my great kindness toward the birds did I forego the Doughnuts that were on the table at Breakfast, and now behold the reward of my Virtue.

And I said, I would I could claim much greater credit than I do for my benevolence, but whatever credit there is coming to me, I take it with the Doughnuts.

And Keturah said, I think it well for thee to save up for thyself all the virtuous credits that come to thee, for indeed thou hast need of them. And in this case I think thou art entitled to some credit. For look now out of the window, and thou shalt see what I did with the Doughnuts which thou rejected.

And I looked out of the window, and behold those Doughnuts lay upon the frozen earth, and every one of them was surrounded by a ring of Birds.

And after that, I ate another of Keturah's Doughnuts. And believe me, they were Some Doughnuts. ❧

Grandpa
and the Bow-wow

There is a land which is called Switzerland, and I and Keturah journeyed thither in the Long Ago. And in one of the cities is a Great Pit wherein are Bears. And the Tourists buy Carrots and feed unto the Bears. And around the place are Booths where they sell Picture Post Cards which thou mayest buy and send unto thy friends, showing that thou art in a country where there are Bears, as there verily are in thine own. And over against the Pit are the shops of the Woodcarvers, who sell Wooden Bears. And I purchased one of these, being half as tall as I am, and holding in his Paws a Wooden Ring for the holding of Canes or Umbrellas. And the Bear is in my Study, and holdeth Canes that I have carried in Many Lands.

And all Children love the Bear, for he is Friendly, and his Glass Eyes are Kindly, and no little boy or girl could well be afraid of him. And the Head and Back of the Bear are Smooth with the patting and stroking of Little Children.

Now the daughter of the daughter of Keturah hath a Little Sister, and she is Two Years old. And she is about the Brightest Little Bit of Color that shineth up this old world. And almost every day, when the daughter of the daughter of Keturah and my Little Grandson are in school, then doth the daughter of Keturah come over to see Keturah, and they climb the stair to where I work.

And I hear the little feet climbing the Stair, and a little Voice saying, I want to see Grandpa. Is Grandpa in?

And all the way as she cometh up the Stair, her Single-track mind is full of the idea of Seeing Grandpa.

But the minute she entereth the room, she taketh one good look at Grandpa, and runneth across the room and Huggeth the Bear, whom she calleth a Bow-wow.

And Grandpa is not in the running until she hath caressed the Bow-wow.

Now, if I were a silly old Grandpa, I should feel hurt at this. But I am neither old nor silly, and I do not intend ever to be either. And I Say Nothing but Saw Wood until she hath done with the Bow-wow. Then doth she run to me, and climb into my Lap, and put her Chubby Little Arms around my neck, and say, I love Grandpa.

And I have considered these things, and have remembered mine own conduct.

For verily, I have climbed slowly and with faltering feet up the Stairs of reverence and devotion, saying as I climbed on Stepping Stones of my Dead Self to Higher Things, I would see God. I would know more of mine Heavenly Father. And in this I have been sincere.

And then, as hath happened more than once or twice, I have seen some Trivial yet Pleasant Thing, and I have run unto it, and later have been sorry that I was so Fickle.

Now the Bible doth not say that Little Children are to enter into the kingdom like Grown Folk, which would be a Sad Misfortune, but that Grown Folk are to enter as a Little Child. And this doth Encourage Me.

Wherefore, I pray, saying, O my God, who knoweth our Frame and Rememberest that we are Dust, Thou art more Wise and Just than to judge me Wholly by the way I turn to the right hand or the left in pursuit of this or that Trivial Thing in Life. Thou knowest Mine Heart even as I know the heart of this Chubby, Snuggly Little Lump of Caprice and Affection. Judge me, O my God, as I judge this Little Child, and love me as I love her, and even a Little More. And have Mirthful Mercy on the shortcomings of Thy Fickle Children, for, Lord, we love Thee more than these. ❦

The Dummy
Organ Pipe

Now it came to pass as I journeyed, that I came upon a Great Church, which the Builders were making Greater. And they pulled down a certain portion of the Wall, and builded it Westward, and they removed the Organ, and builded one Greater. Now, the Organ that had been within the church had been sweet of tone, but it was deemed Too Small, and, moreover, it had grown Rickety, so that it Creaked, and Squawked, and did those things which it Ought Not to have done, and left undone the Things which it Ought to have done. Wherefore they removed it. But the Pipes therein were still good, and they Saved them with Care, to be builded into another and a Greater Organ.

Now, the old Organ had neer been so great as it seemed, but had been Builded into a Larger Space than it could Occupy. And one-half of the Pipes in the Front Row were Real Pipes and the other Half were Dummies. And the organ had stood for forty years, and no man sitting in front of it could have told that Half the Pipes were Dummies, nor could he have told which were the Real Pipes, and which were the Dummies.

But when the Organ was removed, the Real Pipes were Packed with Care, and sent away to a Great Factory, there to be Rebuilded into some other Organ. But the Dummy Pipes, some larger and some smaller, were cast into the junk to be hauled away into the Valley of Hinnom, which same is a valley outside the city gates, like unto that which is near Jerusalem, where the worm dieth not, because it feedeth ever upon refuse, and the fire is not quenched, because ever they haul to it more junk.

Now as the Dummy Pipes waited for the coming of the Trash Man, to haul them to the Valley of Hinnom, one of the workmen took the largest of the pipes, which was Twelve Cubits long, and was like unto a Real Pipe which might have given forth the tone of Middle C in the Open Diapason, but which had never given forth a tone, for it was a Dummy. And the Workman took it, and placed it at the end of a Sewer Pipe, for the same had been broken apart in the building; yet the Sewer was still in use in the older part of the Sanctuary, but there was need for certain days that a Temporary Pipe should be placed there, lest the Filth should Run out in the place where workmen wrought; and there was more work that had to be done before the Plumbers could make the Sewer Connection. So I came and beheld, and Lo, the Beautiful Pipe, that was Twelve Cubits in Length, and Half a Cubit broad, was in use as a drain for the Drainage of Filth.

And I was displeased, and I sought out the Master of the Workmen, and I said, What do ye, defiling a Pipe that hath had its place in the Organ? Surely ye have done an Unholy thing!

And he said, That pipe is doing good service, and it had been thrown away, and it was good for nothing else. Wherefore should we spend money and have the work delayed, to buy a Pipe when here is one at our Hand that is Big Enough, and Long enough for our needs?

Nay, said I, but not this Pipe. For this hath had its part in the Worship of the House of God; and even though it be cast aside I would have it treated Reverently.

But the Master of the Workmen spake to me sternly, and he said, Business is Business. Take heed to thy Preaching and I will attend to my Building. We must use what Material we can from the Old Building to save us Money on the New. For what with the High Cost of Living, and the peril of Strikes, it is hard enough to pay Expenses as it is.

Then said I, Lo, I am a poor man, yet will I pay for a Sheet Iron Pipe for that place, that a Thing be not Defiled with Filth that hath had a place in the worship of God.

But the Master Builder said to me, Keep thy Money, and be not too free with it. As for the Pipe, trouble not thyself. Forty years it stood in the House of God, falsely proclaiming itself to give forth sweet Music, and it gave none. This is the first time since it was made that it hath ever been of Any Use under Heaven. Let it be used for the One Thing it is good for, and then let it go with the Junk.

Then I went my way, and I meditated, and I said, Lo, this is the portion of the Hypocrite; for though he stand in his place in the House of God for Forty years, yet at the end shall he appear as a Hollow Mockery, and God shall find for him whatever Place he still can be of use, but it may not be a Pleasant Occupation.

And many times thereafter I thought about the Dummy Organ Pipe, and the Dummy Christian. And I said, Lo, if it must be that anyone whose life was a Sham shall go to the Valley of the Sons of Hinnom, the ways of the Lord are just and righteous altogether.

But I remembered that the Dummy Pipe was Decorated with Gold Leaf, and it was good to look upon. And I sorrowed at the base use to which it was put. But I could not deny that It was useful at the end.

And I considered these things. ❧

Assisting
the Burglars

It hath been the custom in our home that the children should put on their Nighties and kneel down at the knees of Keturah and say their Prayers before they went to bed. And this I did also at my mother's knees, and likewise did Keturah at the knees of her mother.

And our children said each of them, Now I Lay Me, which is a Poem that some silly folk think is unsuited to Modern Children. But if they will bring up any better Children on their milk-and-water stuff than were brought up on Now I Lay Me, I shall be glad. But after they had said Now I lay me, each one of our five children would say a Prayer of his Own. And they prayed each one after his or her own heart. And there are few finer memories to Keturah and me than our Five Children in their nighties all offering their Evening Prayers. And however much their prayers were unlike those of Grown Folk, Keturah reproved them not. For those folk are wrong who would say unto children, Unless ye become as Stupid and Commonplace as Grown Folk ye shall not enter into the Kingdom of Heaven; for the dear Lord Jesus said it just the other way around.

Now there was one of our sons who was always finding Lame Dogs and bringing them home, and he prayed ever for the Birdies that get Hurted, and for the Dogs that go lame and have none to help them, and for all men and women and children who suffer.

But now and then as he prayed, he remembered that many of the folk who suffer bring their suffering upon themselves by their own folly and sin. And with them in mind, he would end his prayer, saying, And I can't help the Burglars, and Amen.

The years have come and gone, and I have looked out over the world, and have often found relief in the same Disclaimer of Responsibility. And I say, O Lord, thy judgments are true and righteous altogether, but there is much in this world that is Mighty Perplexing. Sin and Folly account for most of the pain in this world, but not all; and if Thou, Lord, shouldest mark iniquity, who should stand in thy sight? I have been Praying and Boosting and Uplifting and Reforming for a Good Long Time, and the job seemeth as big as ever. Lord, there cometh a point where I am not able to Assume Responsibility for all that happeneth in this Mixed-up World. Still do I pray for the needy and the sorrowing and the sinful. Still do I count a part of mine own interest in life all that hath human interest. But, Lord, this Proposition is a Little Too Big for me, and now and then I feel as Doctor Martin Luther felt when he spake unto the Sainted Philip Melancthon, saying, Philip, for this day we will leave the Governance of the Universe with God, and thou and I will Go Fishing. And I think of the sins and sorrows of human life, and say, Lord, I will bear on my sympathies all that one Human Heart can stand up under, and continue the March Around Jericho, but I can't help the Burglars, and Amen. 𑇛

The Uses of the White Elephant

Now the Women of the City where I live sought how they might secure a sum of money for a Children's Hospital, and they devised a White Elephant Sale. And the meaning of the words was this, that when any Woman had in her house something which she wished to Get Rid Of, she called it a White Elephant, and she gave it to the Sale.

Now as I walked in the City, I drew nigh unto the place, and I went within. And there were Books and Bonnets and Baskets, and Clothes and Candlesticks, and Pots and Pictures, and divers kinds of Tools, and Many Things of Other Sorts. And a Damsel said to me, Wilt thou not buy of me something? And in her Booth were Earthen Vessels and Vessels of Brass. And she said, Behold this Lovely Vase. Thou couldest not buy it at Marshall Field's for Fourteen Dollars, but here it is Only a Dollar.

And I took from my purse a Dollar, and she wrapped the Vase in the Part of an old Newspaper that hath Colored Pictures, and I bore it Home.

And my wife, Keturah, met me at the door, and she spake to me and said, Whence comest thou, and what dost thou bring?

And I said, I come from the White Elephant Sale, and I have brought to thee a Lovely Present.

And I set the Vase upon the Table, and removed the Covering, and Keturah looked upon the Vase, and her countenance fell; and then she laughed.

And I answered and said unto her, Wherefore dost thou laugh?

And she said, Safed, dost thou remember the Hopkins family that lived nigh unto us when we were first married?

And I said, Yea, I remember them, to my sorrow.

And she said, Dost thou not remember that the first of all the evil things they did to us was the Present they Wished on us at our Wedding? Dost thou remember what it was?

And my heart fell within me, and I answered, I think it was a Vase, but Very Unlike This One.

And she laughed again, till she wept. And she said, Safed, Twenty years hath that Horrid Vase been in our Attic, and I never had a chance to Get Rid of it till Yesterday, when I sent it to the White Elephant Sale. And now, behold, thou hast brought it back again.

And again she laughed.

But some women would have scolded.

Now after that I had returned from the White Elephant Sale, there were certain days wherein I feared Lest Keturah should speak to me concerning it, and I hoped that she would not. For there was not much that I could say; and while I love to hear her laugh, still her Laughter concerning the White Elephant Vase had been Immoderate, and I had heard Enough of it. But she spake no more of it, for she is a Wise Woman, and when she hath Laughed, she doth not Rub It In.

But I Looked about the House, where she had put it. And I found it not, neither in the Pantry nor in the Parlor; neither in the Attic nor in the Ashcan. And I said, She hath given it to the Salvation Army. But she cared too much for the Salvation Army to have done such a thing.

Now there was a day when the Apple Blossoms were out, and the Trees were Glorious with them. And Keturah made a Great Bouquet of them, and placed it on the Dinner Table, and it was a Mountain of Fragrant Beauty. And it came down on every side so that it touched the Table. And I praised her, for she had done Excellently.

And on the Third Day she said, Behold, the Petals have fallen, and the Bouquet is no longer Beautiful. Wilt thou not carry it out, and Throw it Away?

And I did even as she asked me. And when I had thrown the stems away, I looked at the Vase in my hand, and it was even the White Elephant.

And I was minded to take it, and throw it into the Lake. But she Restrained me.

And she said unto me, Even though the Vessel be unlovely, yet doth it Hold Water, yea and Hold flowers; and I can drape the Flowers that they Cover the Vase, that only the Beauty shall Appear.

And I said, Oh, Keturah, thou art a wonder; but why not cast it away, and buy a Vase that is Beautiful?

And she said, I have decided to keep it that it may be to us a Parable. For everyone hath his White Elephant, and life bringeth to all men and women much of which they fain would be rid, yet which the Providence of God permitteth them not to cast wholly out of their lives. And when they find that it is so, lo, there is a way, if they seek for it, whereby they may Make the Best of it. Even so have I resolved to do with my White Elephants.

And I meditated long. And I spake, saying, Keturah.

And she smiled and said, Say on.

And I asked her, Am I one of thy White Elephants?

And she smiled yet more, and she said, Whether thou art or not, no Mark Down Sale shall have thee.

Sunset on Main Street

I visited a land called Indiana, and I sat on the Porch of the City Hotel that fronteth on Main Street at the time of the going down of the Sun. And there sat with me an Habitant of that Village, and I remarked concerning the Beauty of the Sunset. Now I verily believe that he had never thought of it before, but his Bosom Swelled with Pride, and he said:

For a town of its size, this City hath as Fine Sunsets as can be seen anywhere in all this Broad and Happy Land.

Now I rather liked that man, for albeit he had not noticed the Sunset until I had spoken thereof, yet was he quick to Appropriate it and claim it for his Own Town. And I fully agreed with him, that, so far as I know, there is no town of its size that hath more Glorious Sunsets than his town.

This I notice when I visit other Cities, that my friends there are determined that my feet shall not press the soil of those communities; for they bring Automobiles to mine Inn, and take me on Long Drives, and this is a custom to be Encouraged. And if Keturah be with me, so much the more is it Desirable that they take us Driving.

But I am not so much for Pleasant Drives that get us

nowhere, nor of long and pleasant roads that lead to nothing. Neither do I care much to have pointed out to me the Ninth Largest Ford Assembling Plant in the world, nor the Fourteenth Largest Storage Warehouse in Christendom, nor the Third Largest Factory for the making of Chewing Gum. But for those who work for Mr. Ford, and for those who move the Furniture, and for those who Chew the Gum, for them do I care. And if there be those who Chew no Gum, for them do I care yet more.

For Human Life is the measure of Value, even the Value of the Sunset. Suns and moons and worlds are of value only as they impart meaning and value to Life. And the Sunset is none too glorious for Main Street. I would that all the dwellers on Main Street would consider how glorious it is, and how gloriously life may be lived, even in a city that hath little to boast about save only its Sunsets and its quality of Human Life. &

The Man from Jonesville

Now, there was among my Neighbors a man whose name was Smith, and he was from Jonesville. And he told me often of Jonesville, what a Lovely Place it was, and how every one who lived there was Happy and Virtuous, and how sorry he was that he ever had left there, and how he wanted to go back to Jonesville. And when the men in the city where I lived failed to clean the Snow off their Sidewalks, or the City Council indulged in Graft, or the children were Rude, or there was an Early Frost, he told me that Such Things did not happen in Jonesville. And this continued for nigh unto Twenty Years; and the older he grew the more he talked about Jonesville. And I told him I hoped that when he died he would go to Jonesville.

Now it came to pass that he prospered, so that he retired from Business. And he sold his House and Lot in the City wherein I dwell, and went back to Jonesville that he might Spend his Last Years in Peace, and Die in Jonesville. And we all Bade him Farewell, with something of Sorrow, and Something of Relief.

And it came to pass that at the end of Six Months, he and his Wife moved back again, and bought back their Old House for a Thousand Dollars more than they sold it for.

And they were Tenfold more Happy to get back than they had been to go away.

And it came to pass on an Evening that Keturah and I called on them, I said, Old Fellow, tell me on the Level, what was the matter with Jonesville?

And he said to me, Speak not to me of Jonesville, lest I do thee Harm. It is the toughest Joint this side of States Prison. The dear people we knew have all died or moved away, and they who are in their places are Unneighborly and Snobbish. And they Tango and do other Outrageous Stunts, and their Kids are the Limit. We have come back to Dwell in the place where we have spent Twenty Happy Years, and we have but one favor to ask of our old Neighbors, and that is, that they never speak to us of Jonesville.

And as Keturah and I walked home, I spake to her, and said, Keturah.

And Keturah answered, I know what thou art about to say; and I suspected all the time that it would be just so.

And I said, There are many men and women who sigh for some Jonesville or other, who might be Decently Happy where they are if they would make it their business.

And Keturah said, Our Jonesville is right here.

And I said, Amen. 🙰

Keturah
and the Flowers

I am an Occasional and Unsuccessful Gardener. But I raise Hollyhocks. And when they be once planted they continue. For the old plants die the Second Winter, but the young ones bear in the Second Summer. And I like to remember how the Crusaders when they went to the Holy Land brought back this Glorious Blossoming Scepter to the Gardens of Europe and to my garden and that of Keturah.

But Keturah is more industrious than I. She planteth Flowers of divers kinds.

And it came to pass that she set out Flowers, and Rude Boys came by in the night and pulled them up.

And Keturah suspected who they were.

Now it came to pass on a day that Keturah saw that Tough Bunch coming. And she took a Basket of Apples that she had ready, and she went out into the Porch. And she saluted them as they were passing by, and they answered her Gruffly, and edged away, for they feared that she would Bawl them Out or threaten them with the Police.

And Keturah said unto them, What tall, manly fellows ye are. How strong ye are, and how brave.

And by that she had them Guessing.

And she said, I need help from you, and I am sure that

you will give it. I plant flowers, and boys pull them up. They are not bad boys, but thoughtless. I desire that you help me to protect my Flowers.

And they said nothing.

And she said, I have boys, and they also are strong and tall. And they have grown up and gone forth into the world. I am as old as the mothers of you boys, and it is hard work to set out Flowers and have them plucked up. And I know that if you boys, who are so strong and brave, will protect my Flowers, and speak to the other boys about them, then my Flowers will Grow and Blossom.

And when she had said this, she produced her Apples.

Now thus it hath been ever since the Wind and the Sun had their quarrel as to which could compel a man to take off his Coat; and the stronger the Wind blew, the more he tightened it, but the warmth of the Sun quickly accomplished what the harsh treatment could not do.

And if thou shalt pass the Garden of Keturah, thou shalt find her Flowers unmolested. For they are guarded by the best policemen in town, even by the boys.

There be those whose word of progress is, Treat them Rough; but Keturah can show unto you a More Excellent Way. ❧

The Flower Catalogue

Now the Storms of Winter blew Cold, and the Snow of Winter lay Deep, when the mails brought a Catalogue of Flower Seeds and Bulbs. And Keturah opened it, and gazed therein with Great Admiration. And she said, Safed.

And I answered, Here Am I, Keturah.

And she said, Didst thou ever see Flowers so Beautiful as these in this Catalogue?

And I answered, Neither have I seen such nor has any another person; such flowers are not in Nature, but in Art.

Nevertheless, said she, I like to look on them, and some of them will I buy.

And I said, Behold the house wherein we live is not our own, and it lately was a Place of Weeds, and there is a Row of Flats hard by.

But she said, We will make it More Attractive. Thou hast thy Hollyhocks; I will have Phlox and Chrysanthemums and Cockleshells and Silver Bells and Cowslips all in a Row.

So she wrote to the one whose Vivid Imagination had produced the Catalogue, and sent Money, and he wrote that he would send the Plants in the Spring.

And it came to pass on a day that they came by

Express. And I digged in the Ground with a Spade, and I set them out that they should grow. And the Roots were wondrous things wherewith to lay hold on the Earth and transform it into Beauty, so that the one kind of Root might make earth and water into Roses, and another into Lilies. And as I digged in the Earth I thought much of the Wonder of Life as God had placed it in the world.

And I said to her, Keturah, we might not have done this had not some Benefactor of the Human Race sent us a Seed Catalogue.

And she said, Told I not thee it would be well that we should do this?

And I answered, Whether we tarry here a year or ten years, still am I glad to have planted some Flowers. Yea, though we live not to enjoy them, yet will others be glad. Keturah, thou has done well. And so did the one who sent the Catalogue.

And I called down from Heaven a Blessing upon all, be they Ministers or Merchants, who suggest to folk the good things they ought to do, and who make the doing of them Lovely.

For I myself am a distributor of Catalogues of Assorted Virtues, and I say to people, Behold how lovely is Goodness! Go to, even now in the Winter of thy Depravity, and break up the fallow ground of thy heart against the time when thou shalt plant goodness, and it shall Blossom in Beauty. ❧

The Plant
I Did Not Buy

Now while I was setting out the Roots which Keturah had bought from the one who made the Seed Catalogue, I found one root that Stuck up out of the Ground, and I laid hold upon it, and I said, Here is a Root that Beareth no Label. I wonder what it is. Behold, I know not, yet will I plant it, and see what Cometh up.

And Keturah answered and said, Knowest thou not what that is? It is a Dandelion which thou didst Dig up in making the Holes for the Flowers.

And I was ashamed that I had not known it before. Nevertheless, I saw what it was, even while she was telling me. For I am not wholly Ignorant, albeit for the moment I knew not the root, what it was.

And I held the Dandelion root in my hand. And I looked at it, and beheld how Deep it had sunk into the Earth, and how firmly it had laid hold on the Soil with its one long Root, and I admired the way it had planned to Stay Put.

And I looked at the top, and though it seemed to have no life, yet there were Leaves Curled up and ready to push themselves forth, yea, and a Bud that was all but ready to lift its head above the ground as soon as the winter was past.

And I said to the Dandelion, Behold thou art a Plucky Plant. Thou sinkest thy Root to a Great Depth. Thou sendest up thy Hollow Stalk in the form of Construction the Strongest known to any Engineer. Thy White Ball of soft Down is the most Beautiful and Delicate thing in Nature; yea, and even thy Yellow Blossom is Marvelous, for every little yellow leaf is a flower. Moreover, it is not thy fault that folk call thee a Weed. If it were only Hard to make thee Grow, we would pay Good Money for thy Roots, and break our Backs setting thee out, and declare that a sight of thee, sprinkling thy gold over a green Lawn, was the Perfection of Gardening. Neither didst thou sin nor thy parents, yet art thou Despised and Rejected, and good folk Love thee Not.

And when I thought of these things, I could not find it in my heart to cut off a life so wonderful and so plucky; neither did I want it in my garden. But I took it down to the Alley that runneth behind my house, and I planted it there. And I said, Now the Lord judge whether it be not better thou shouldst grow there than that the ground be cumbered by a Tin Can.

Yet I looked around and hastened back to the House lest my Neighbors should know that I had planted a Dandelion.

And who knoweth whether I did right or wrong?

For if some great Blight should come upon the Dandelions in the Front Lawns of all peoples, then would they come and seek in my Alley, and beg a seed of my Dandelion.

For though I be chided for giving the Dandelion a Fighting Chance for its life, yet have I known those whose lives were as Weeds whom God Spared in His Mercy, and they Bloomed in Wonderful and Unexpected Goodness.

The Weeds
in My Garden

Now, after I had planted my Garden, there were certain mornings when I rose early and took my Hoe, and went out, and Watched Things Grow. And my soul was Enlarged.

But as it grew later in the Spring there came nights when I had been out, and the Morning Came Too Soon, and I went not into my Garden. And when I went after a Week or Two, behold the Weeds had grown Faster than my Plants.

And I toiled with my Hoe till I blistered my Hand, yet gained I but little. And Everything seemed to Happen to my Plants, and nothing to harm the Weeds.

And one day I returned from my Garden, and I was weary. And I ate my bread in the sweat of my face.

And I said, O Keturah, I am a Punk Gardener.

And Keturah answered, It would not be becoming in me to Dispute my husband.

And I said, Behold, my fathers before me were Punk Gardeners. My first Ancestor was a Gardener, and he could not Hold Down his Job.

And Keturah answered, Do not be Discouraged overmuch. That Ancestor of thine Got some Good Things out of his Garden; surely thou canst do as well as he.

And I answered, Yea, he got some good things out of that Garden, the one of which was Experience; and that is a fruit that hath its bitter and its sweet, but is Profitable.

And Keturah answered, You have spoken wisely. Likewise did Adam get a vision of the Eternal Mystery of Life, and beheld the wonder of Nature, that seed cast into the ground cometh forth in marvelous forms of beauty. Oh, Safed, is not that worth a blistered hand?

And I answered, O thou wise woman, thou speakest wisely and well; for Adam and Eve learned how to be workers together with God.

Then were we silent for a season, for we thought of many strange and wondrous things that we had seen in our Garden.

And I said, Keturah.

And she said, Speak on.

And I said, Adam got one other good thing out of his Garden.

And she said, What was that?

And I said, It was the most Enjoyable, yet the most Troublesome.

And she said, Thou speakest in riddles, Surely thou dost not mean the serpent?

And I spake thus, The fairest flower that bloomed in Eden was no other than Eve.

And Keturah said nothing, and I made as if I had nothing more to say; but she knew I would say more. Therefore was she silent.

And I said, Keturah, I have a choice blossom from that same vine. Neither I nor Adam have failed wholly in the care of our Gardens. ❧

The Flower
in the Obstruction

Now it came to pass in one of my journeys that I lodged with a Friend who in former years did Preach, but now hath Retired, and liveth in a goodly Little City wherein is a College, and where in former years he Preached. And he hath bought for himself an House, situated where two streets cross, and he liveth Happily and Quietly and Usefully. Even so may the Lord grant me Grace and Cash wherewith to live when I come to his time of life.

Now, the boys of the city pass his home on their way to School, and divers of them turn the Corner there; and having learned from a certain teacher called Euclid, whose theories no man disputeth because few Understand Them, that the Square on the Hypotenuse is equal to the Square upon the other two sides, and having some doubt about it, they create an Hypotenuse across the Lawn of my friend, in order to find if it be not true that the Hypotenuse is shorter than the way around the Corner.

Now, the Neighbors of my Friend spake unto him, saying:

Those Infernal Boys will Ruin thy Lawn. Go to, Make a Stumbling Block in their Path, and make it of Barb Wire, that they entangle themselves therein and be pricked with the Goads, and cease to ruin thy front Yard.

So my Friend built a Stumbling Block and placed it in their Path, but of Barb Wire builded he not. He built it of stone, and filled it in with earth, and he dug it, and dunged it, and therein he planted flowers.

And the boys thereafter kept to the walk, and they looked at the flowers and admired them, and they spake:

Lo, the Good Man hath planted a Flower Bed in his Lawn; now Shall we Keep on the Walk lest we injure it; and to walk around it were more Bother than to Keep in the Great Highway.

And the Boys never suspected that it was for their sake he planted the Flowers, nor that the Flowers were planted to Beautify the Bunker.

Now, when I beheld this, I said to my soul:

Behold, my Friend is not only a person of kind heart, but also a Man of Great Wisdom. How easily he might have wakened the resentment of the Youthful Soul, whereas he hath gladdened the heart of the neighborhood, saved his Lawn and kept the good will of the Boys.

Then I thought of the many Stumbling Blocks which good folk have erected in the Path of the Sinful, and how often they have become futile, for I have beheld Youth Vaulting happily over the Barbed Wire, and landing with his Heels deep in the turf on the farther side. And I said to my soul:

Whenever it is necessary to erect a hurdle across the path of the wicked or the thoughtless, I will seek out a Flower and plant thereon. And the same shall be reckoned unto me for Righteousness as well as practical Good Sense.

The Guest-Room Towels

There came to me one who said, The trouble with thee, and with the Church, and with all who labor with thee, is that thy Methods are Old. We are living in a New Age, and the Old Methods are Inadequate.

And I answered, Thou speakest truly, and perhaps wisely.

And he said, How is it that if what I say is Certainly True it is only Possibly Wise?

And I answered him, Because there are no kinds of unwisdom so great as those that are founded on Truth that is Ill Considered. What New Methods dost thou advocate?

And he Got Busy with a Line of Talk about his New Methods, that never had been tried anywhere, and which were certain of but one thing, that they never would work.

And he said, How dost thou like my New Methods?

And I said unto him,

I went to a certain city, and lodged with a friend who sent me to my bed in the Guest Chamber. And it was a Comfortable Chamber, and he had made it ready for my coming. And among the other Preparations, he had hung the towel-rack full of New Linen Towels, which he had purchased by the Dozen, and there were Six of them in my

Room. And they were Very Nice Towels, and well worth the Price that he paid, for Linen was Going Up. But when I essayed to wipe my face upon them, I could not do it. For those Towels were every one of them as Stiff and as Shiny as a Sheet of Tin, and likewise as Impervious to Water. So I mussed them up, one of them and yet another and another till I had polished my face with the Metalic Surface of all six of them.

And I said unto him, There must needs be New Methods, and I would not be last in the use of any of them that are good. Neither do I care to be the first to dry my face upon a New Towel. Let him that is ambitious for a New Experiment try it before me, and after it hath gone to the Laundry and come back, less Shiny but more Serviceable, then will I try it. It is enough for me that I must wear my own New Boots. &

The Fish
and the Bait

There were in a certain city two boys. And they both loved to fish. And there came a day when the Spring was alluring, and they listened unto the Call of the Wild. And they went out of the city, and sat them down by a Certain Stream. And they essayed to fish.

But one of these boys before he went, took a Tomato Can and an Hoe, and went into the Back Yard, and dug until he had a Dozen Worms and a Blister. But the other boy liked to fish and did not like to Dig Worms.

And it came to pass at the end of the day, that they returned home both of them. But one of them had a string of fish and a Sunburnt Nose, and the other had only a Sunburnt Nose.

And it came to pass that those two boys grew into Manhood. And one of them before he began any New Enterprise, went into the Back Yard of the matter, and did a lot of hard digging. And the other just shouldered his pole and went into the affair, and watched his Cork placidly floating upon the Surface of the Stream, and never going under. And the history of one of these men was a Succession of Successes, and the other was a Series of Sheriff's Sales.

And when I considered these matters, I said, Life is a Fish Pond, but it is more than that. It is also a Back Yard out of which Worms are to be digged with much Arduous Toil; and other things being equal, one's String of Fish is proportioned unto the Size of his Tin Can of Bait, and the number of blisters in his hands that were made by the Hoe Handle.

For while the Hoe Handle is less pleasant to the hand than the Fishing Pole, it is an Important Element in the successful catching of Fish. ✷

The
Bubbles

The daughter of the daughter of Keturah is now an important young lady of nine years, and she can read and write, and play a number of pieces on the Piano. But the Little Sister of the daughter of the daughter of Keturah is two. And she is about the brightest spot of color on the Map. And I have seen Keturah catch her up, as she was running about in a Blue Dress, with her Red-Gold hair flying, and her eyes two little spots of Heaven, and her cheeks as red as Roses, and Keturah hath said, Such a Little Animated Doll as thou art is not Possible.

Now the daughter of the daughter of Keturah provided herself with a Bowl of Soap Suds and a Pipe, and she sat upon the floor, Blowing Bubbles. And the Little Sister of the daughter of the daughter of Keturah sat over against her upon the floor. And the daughter of the daughter of Keturah blew Bubbles that were Large and Iridescent and Beautiful, and she dropped them on the head of her Little Sister. And her Little Sister was Delighted.

And after about a Dozen or a Score of Bubbles had been dropped upon her head, the Little Sister put up her hand to take them all down that she herself might behold them.

For she supposed that the Bubbles were still All There, in an Heap the size of a Peck Measure upon the top of her head.

And when she put up her hand, behold, all the Bubbles had broken save one, and she broke that one in reaching for it.

And she was Astonished, and would have Wept. But the daughter of the daughter of Keturah laughed, and blew another Bubble, and her Little Sister laughed, too, albeit rather solemnly.

And when I beheld this, I said unto Keturah, The whole More or Less Human Race is like unto that Little Damsel. For men and women are always Fooling Themselves with the notion that all the Soap Bubbles they have ever blown were Ponderable and Durable, and behold, it is not so; for they are Frail, and they endure but for a moment.

And Keturah said, But there are Lasting Joys, and it were better if we did seek more of them.

And I said, Thou hast spoken wisely. Yet we cannot spare the Bubbles. There are Durable Blessings and Perishable Blessings, and we need both kinds. But we must use the Perishable Blessings, for the Fashion of this world Passeth Away, as a certain wise man said in a day when Fashions might change perchance once in a Thousand Years, and oftener than that now. The Flowers were not made to last, but to be enjoyed while they are with us. Spring is not made to last. Youth is not made to last.

And Keturah said, Ours is lasting Fairly Well. ❧

The Windmill
and the Pump

I have a friend who is an Husbandman, and I visited him upon his Farm, and tarried with him one night. And upon his Farm are Cattle and Swine and Horses. And he watereth them from a Deep Well wherein is a Pump, and the Pump runneth by a Windmill.

And it came to pass after Supper that he spake unto a Worker that labored upon the farm, and he said: There is a Good Breeze tonight; start thou the Windmill.

And the Worker went forth into the Night, and loosened a Rod that runneth up to the Mill, and that holdeth the Tail against the Wheel so that the Wind driveth it not. But when the Rod is loosened, then the Tail swingeth around, and the Wheel cometh into the Wind, and the Wheel turneth to Beat the Band. And ere the Worker had returned to the house, we heard the Wheel running, and my friend said, On the morrow we shall have a Tank full of Water for the Livestock.

Now the room where I slept was on the side of the house toward the Windmill, and when I wakened in the night, it was Running like the Wind, and I said, Verily it will pump the well dry at that rate.

But when we went out in the morning, behold, there

was no water. For the Pump had been Disconnected from the Mill, and the Worker saw not in the Darkness that the Connecting Pin was out; wherefore he connected it not. And the mill had run all night and the Tank was empty.

Now when I beheld this, I thought of many folk whom I know, whose Windmill goeth around continually, and who are always Creaking their Boots to show that they are Among Those Present, and who talk long and earnestly about Earnestness and Efficiency and the Rest, but it Cutteth no Ice, and it Draweth no Water. Now these be good folk, whose minds are Responsive to the Winds of God, and their Capacity for doing something is as Excellent as that of the Pump, but between the Wheels that God driveth and the Pump of their own endeavor, there lacketh an adjustment.

And I have often wondered how it should be that in the mechanism of some good people there would seem to have been evidenced the blunder of some Sleepy Soul, fumbling in the dark, and putting the Wheel in Gear, but failing to connect the Pump. And this is the word that I spake in the ears of men and women, Count it not a sure sign of efficiency that the Wheel goeth round and the Pump is in order; be thou sure the Wheels of thy Head are hitched to the Pump of thy Performance. ℀

The One-Course Dinner

When I and Keturah had been married for the space of one month, she spake unto me saying, Tonight thy Dinner shall have but One Course, and there shall be enough of it.

So we sat down to eat, and we gave God thanks, and I lifted the cover of the dish, and behold, there was a Short-cake, made of Black berries, for it was the season of that kind of fruit.

And we ate each of us one piece, and Keturah said, That is thy Soup.

And we ate each of us another, and she said, That is thy Fish.

And we ate each of us another, and Keturah gave it the name of another course. And she ate no more. But I ate as long as Keturah could think of the names of more courses. For it was the first time in my life that I had eaten enough of Short-cake.

And when the next Summer came, Keturah did likewise again, save that she did it with Strawberries.

And when she found that I liked Strawberries, but that I like Red Raspberries still better then she did it with Red Raspberries.

And it would be of no use to tell any one else how good

those Short-cakes were. And when we had them, we had nothing else, save the Sugar and the Cream.

And now and again Keturah still maketh for me a Dinner with but One Course, and it sometimes is Flannel Cakes with Hot Maple Syrup, and sometimes it is Hot Biscuits and Red Raspberries, and sometimes it is Hot Corn Bread and Honey.

And at the beginning I was wont to say to her, Keturah, let us have it ever thus.

But I have ceased to say that. For Keturah hath often told me that even the best of meals are better for Variety, and that meals of One Course, and that a mighty good one, are desirable chiefly when they themselves are a variety. And the same is true of many good things in life. For goodness hath often been made unlovely by its Infernal Monotony.

Roller Skates
and Riches

The daughter of the daughter of Keturah came unto me, saying:

My little playmate, Willis, hath a grandpa, and his grandpa hath bought for him a pair of Roller Skates.

And I said, The grandpa of Willis is President of a Bank.

And she inquired, saying, What is the President of a Bank?

And I answered, He is a man who doth accommodate his friends by borrowing their money without Interest and Loaning it back to them at Six Per Cent.

And she asked of me saying, Grandpa, is the grandpa of Willis as rich as you?

And I said, Nay, my dear; for he hath not so many children or grandchildren.

And she said, Shall we go to where they sell Roller Skates?

And I said, We will surely go there, and we will stay not on the order of our going.

So we went to the place where they sell, and we bought the skates.

Now in the days of my youth, when there were no

Movies, and there was no Jazz, there were Skating Rinks, wherein the youth did congregate, and roll around on an Hardwood Floor. But Concrete Pavements were there none, and the young folk did not skate all over Creation as now they do. But I remember that wheels under the feet of youth feel fine.

And as we walked toward home, the little maiden thought much of How Rich she was with her Skates, and How Rich must be her grandpa to buy them, and she remembered that I had spoken of the wealth of the grandfather of her playmate. And she inquired, saying:

Grandpa, is any one in the world more rich than you?

And I thought of my Home and my Health and my Friends and my Children, and my Children's Children, and my Books and my Job. Yea, I remembered that my Check is as good at the Bank for any sum that I have need to draw as that of John D. Rockefeller or the grandfather of Willis, and I said:

No, my little girl, there is no man in the world more rich than thy grandpa. ❧

The
Kid Finger

My little Grandson pinched his finger in the door, so that the Nail was Bruised, and came off. And there came a time when it was Hanging at one end but loose at the other. And his mother called me upon the Telephone, and said, I desire to slip the Finger of a Glove upon it that it may be protected, but he feareth that it will hurt him, and he saith, Nay, but let Grandpa do it.

And I said, Bring him hither.

And I took him upon my knee, and said, First we will clip a part of the old Nail away.

And he said, Nay, for it will hurt.

And I said, Let us watch and see how far the pieces of Nail do fly.

And we watched, and it did not hurt.

But it was not easy to slip the Finger of the Kid Glove upon the Finger of the hand, for the Nail still hung and was tender. And his mother slipped it on by littles, while I sang unto him. And this is the song that I sang:

Oh, a little Kid Finger on the Finger of the Kid,
Will protect the little Finger and will keep the Finger hid;
It will heal the little Finger just the best was ever did;
Oh, the little Kid Finger on the Finger of the Kid!

THE KID FINGER

Now if it be objected that this is not Great Poetry, I answer that it falleth into the category of Occasional Verse, like Coronation Odes, and it is, as I judge, quite as good Poetry as Alfred Lord Tennyson wrote for the Jubilee of Queen Victoria, and somewhat better suited to the occasion that produced it. For the little lad sang with me about the Little Kid Finger on the Finger of the Kid, and before he knew it, the Kid Finger was on tight.

And if anyone would know what Tune this poetry was sung to, it was the Classick melody of the Turkey in the Straw.

For that is Great Poetry which serveth poetickally in a great Need; and that is Great Musick, which in the sphere of Musick functioneth greatly.

And if thou desirest to know my sentiments on the controversy of Art for Art's sake, thou mayest be able to infer it from these Few Remarks. For Musick and Art and all else is Good in proportion as it is Good for Something. And I have very little use for goodness which is good for nothing. ❧

The
Red Card

The daughter of the daughter of Keturah had Measles.
Then came the Board of Health and tacked up a Red Card.
And the daughter of the daughter of Keturah said, We once
had Liberty Bond posters, and then Red Cross posters, and
then Near East posters, and now we have a Measles Card.

And for certain weeks she remained at home, she and
her little brother, and the small baby girl that came lately to
be a joy unto us.

But there fell a day when she came running unto my
Study. And she cried, Grandpa, the Board of Health came
this morning, and took down the Red Card; and Mother
says that I may come and play with you.

Then did I close my book, and go with her.

And we stepped out where the grass was green, and
she said —

See how green and soft the grass is? Would you like to
have me turn some Somersaults?

And I said, Go to it, my dear.

And her golden curls went down into the grass, and
her little heels flew up into the air, and she turned
Somersaults.

And she laughed, and I laughed.

And she said, Grandpa, the Red Card is down; but my little brother has been compared to my Measles and we both have been compared to German Measles and to Whooping Cough. So the Red Card may go back tomorrow, or any day; but This Day is Mine.

When she said that she had been compared I knew that she meant exposed. And I thought that she spake wisely.

And she said, Mother said that she and Grandma were going to Lunch together at a gathering of the women to help somebody, and that I might lunch with you if you invited me.

And I said, Thou art invited. Shall we go unto the Restaurant where we have been before?

And she said, Grandpa, there is a Swell New Restaurant; shall we not go there?

And I said, We will.

And she said, Remember, Grandpa, I have been compared to Whooping Cough and to German Measles, and my little brother has been compared to my Measles, and we know not when the Board of Health will come back, and put up the Red Card again; but This Day is Mine.

And we went to the Swell New Place, and whatsoever the damsel wanted, that did she order; for That Day was Hers.

And this I thought as I considered the matter, that all of us have been compared to a great many uncertainties, neither doth any one of us know what the morrow shall bring forth, nor how soon the Board of Health or something worse may come, nor what shall be nailed up beside the front door. But, beloved, This Day is Ours. This is the Day that the Lord hath made, and the only Day that ever is the Day that is called Today.

This Day is Thine, beloved. Use it, and rejoice in it, and give it over to Love and Service and fail not to find Joy in it; for thou knowest not what shall be on the morrow, and This Day is Thine. ❧

The Weight
of a Tire

I have a friend and he hath an Automobile. And he besought me that I would ride with him, and I did so gladly. And I sat with him in front, and his wife and his daughter sat in the back.

And he stopped at a Garage where he had left a Spare Tire, and they fastened it upon the rear of the Car. For he said, Peradventure we have a Puncture, it is already Inflated, and it hath in it Eighty Pounds of air.

And I asked of him, How much doth the empty Tire weigh?

And he saith, It weigheth Fourteen pounds when it is empty.

And I asked, When it hath in it air with a Pressure of Eighty Pounds, what doth it weigh?

And he said, I know, but we will submit the question to my daughter who goeth unto the High School. If a Tire weigh Fourteen Pounds and have in it Eighty Pounds of air, how much doth it weigh?

And she said, It weigheth Ninety and Four pounds.

And he spake unto his wife and said unto her, This daughter of ours Showeth less Intelligence than I expected.

But his wife said, Eighty pounds and Fourteen pounds are Four and Ninety Pounds, even as our daughter said.

And he laughed at them because they knew not the difference between Air-pressure and Weight.

And I spake unto them, even unto the wife and the daughter, and I said, It is very sinful for a man to make sport of the errors of his wife and his daughter. Moreover, the mistake is not strange. Nevertheless, the air inside the tube doth not greatly increase the weight of the Tube. It still doth weigh Fourteen Pounds, for that within it is only Air, though it press against the Tube it beareth not down upon the Scales.

And they reproached themselves because they had not known.

But I said unto them, Be not discomfited. Behold, many persons have made the same mistake. Yea, it would be well to remind all Preachers when they inflate their sermons, that there is very little weight in Wind. ✼

The
Bad Temper

There came unto me one who said, I have a Very Bad Temper.

And he said it with what he thought was Humility, but it was as it had been a certain sort of Pride.

And I said, Thou art a Narrow-Minded Man.

Then he was angry, and I knew that he was no Liar when he said that he had a Bad Temper.

And when he had said More or Less, I silenced him, and said, I believe thee when thou saidest that thou hadst a Bad Temper; I did not ask thee to make such a Display of it.

And he said, Thou hast Insulted me; for a Quick Temper is not the sign of a Narrow Mind, but of a Warm and Generous Nature: for if I am quick to be angry I am quick also to get over it, and very ready to Make Amends.

Now we spake in the Garden, and I left him for a moment, and when I returned I had been in the Kitchen, and I brought back an Egg.

And I threw the Egg at the Back Fence, and it Brake and spattered the Fence.

And I said, Thou speakest of Making Amends. Gather up that Egg again, and clean off the Fence, and put the Egg back into the Shell, and set an Hen upon it, and make of it a Plymouth Rock Rooster. Then talk to me of Making Amends for thine outbursts of Temper. For thou spatterest over all thy friends, and splashest them with thy fury, and then thou dost leave them to clean off thy rage and try to forget thine unreasonable words, and thou thinkest thou hast Made Amends.

And I said, The best way to Make Amends for a Bad Temper is to keep thy temper to thyself.

And he said, Verily thou didst say of me that I had a Narrow Mind, and I will take that from no one.

And I said, Thou wilt take it once again from me. Thou hast a Narrow Mind. He who hath a Bad Temper is a person who is capable of seeing but one aspect of a thing at a time, and incapable of withholding his snap judgment until he may learn the whole truth. And because he is both narrow-minded and childish, therefore doth he fly into a rage, as thou hast done and habitually dost do. Flatter not thyself that this is the sign of a generous nature, for I have told thee already of what it is a sign.

And he was silent.

And I went and got out the Hose, and started to wash off the Egg from the Fence.

And he would not have it so, but caught the Nozzle from my hand and himself washed off the Egg from the Fence.

And he said—

Though I be not able to produce a Plymouth Rock Rooster from that Egg, yet hath it not been wholly wasted.

And I am inclined to think that he had Learned Something that was worth the price of an Egg.

And I should like to buy some more of them and teach to other men, and some women, the Same Lesson. ❧

The Little Girl
in the Blue Dress

I rode upon a Train from New York even unto Chicago.
And the Train was Full. And among the rest was there a
Young Mother with a Little Girl. And they were going unto
South Bend and the little damsel wore a Blue Dress.

And the little maiden and I became friends; for Little
Girls like me, and I do verily believe that Good Little Girls
are made of Sugar and Spice and all that is Nice.

And she had Dominoes wherewith to play. And she sat
with me, and we set up the Dominoes to make Beds. And
we made of them Single Beds, and Double Beds, and we
tried to make Beds such as were in the Train, but we did not
succeed very well.

And we had ridden all night and much of the day, and
it drew toward evening. And I said, This place is Elkhart,
and the miles unto Chicago are an Hundred and One; and
here do they cut off the Dining Car, and it is our last long
stop. And we shall reach Chicago in Two Hours and
Twenty Minutes, and South Bend will be before that.

And she said, I would that South Bend were farther.

And I inquired of her why she said so.

And she said, There will be Very Hard Letters to learn
in South Bend.

And I said, Why dost thou think there will be Hard Letters to learn?

And she said, I had just begun to go to school when my father got a new job in South Bend and sent for us. And I learned A and B and C all the way down to X and Y and Z, and how to spell CAT and DOG and COW and many more. And my mother says that now I must begin all over again. And the Letters will be different; and who knoweth how they spell COW in South Bend?

And I said, Fear not. They spell it mostly with a C, and only a few of them begin it with a K.

And she said, It will all be so different, and I fear it. I wish this old Train would go on and on, and never come to South Bend.

And I saw that the little maiden was sore distressed by reason of the Very Hard Letters.

And I said unto her, Fear not, my dear. I have been in South Bend, yea, I have passed through it an hundred times. The letters there are A and B and C, and X and Y and Z, and there are twenty-six of them and no more.

And she inquired, Art thou sure?

And I said, Sure thing. And CAT and DOG are the same as in New York, and all that thou didst learn there will be good in South Bend.

And the little maiden was comforted.

Now this hooting, whanging train of human life moveth swiftly; and ever and anon there getteth on some passenger who wondereth how it will be in the place to which he journeyeth, and who approacheth life's destination with fear. And I prayed unto my God that he would send unto all such some of his Experienced Angels, who would say to all such timid souls, Fear not. The Alphabet of Heaven is the kindly deeds and gracious words which thou hast learned in the Kindergarten of Life. Heaven and Earth

have a Common Alphabet, and all that thou hast learned
will be of value there.

And the little maiden flung a kiss toward me as the
Train pulled out of South Bend, and I beheld her in the
arms of her father. ৪৪

The Last
Postage Stamp

And Keturah spake unto me, saying, Hast thou any Postage Stamps?

And I said, I have none here, but I have some in my Study.

And she said, I wish thou wouldst take some letters for me, and see thou forget not to mail them. Three weeks is the limit for thee to carry these Letters in thy Pocket.

And I said, My dear, I am not sure why Delilah delivered Samson over to the Philistines, but I think he had forgotten to mail her letters. I will be careful and remember. But how is it thou art out of Stamps?

And she said, I was sure I had some; for in my drawer was an Whole Strip of what I thought were Stamps upside down. But when I went to get some Stamps, behold there was not a Stamp there. Only there was a long strip of Perforated paper that had been torn off the margin of a sheet of stamps. And instead of Ten Stamps there were Ten Scraps of paper.

And I said, There are few disappointments so great in life as that of going to the Stamp Box in confident expectation, and finding the Last Stamp gone, and the Post Office Closed.

And she said, It would not be so bad if it had not been that there were in the Box those papers that looked like Stamps.

Now I thought of this, and I considered the disappointment of Keturah, how those Blank Stamps were a Delusion and an Hollow Mockery and a Snare. Whereas, had they not been there, she had said, cheerfully, Yes, we have no Postage Stamps, and straightway gone and bought some or asked her Husband to bring some Across.

Now this is the Sad Thing in Human Experience, not that there are no men, and not that there are no women, but that when the time cometh when there have seemed to be men and women enough for any possible event, whole rows and sheets of them are good for nothing and worse than nothing because they create a false sense of security. For they lack what the Perforated Blanks lacked, the stamp of Personality and Authority and Power upon the one side, and the Glue of Tenacity of Purpose upon the other.

Now I thought of this, and I remembered the bitter words of the Prophet concerning the sorrows of God, that He looked for someone to stand in the Gap, and though there were people enough, there were none that had the Picture and the Glue. And I think this must have been the Sorrow of God in all ages. For God hath sometimes stood with an Handful of Righteous Purposes for the which He would have sent one great Event to Spokane and another to Santa Fe and another to Skowhegan, but He could not do many mighty works there or in any of those places.

So the cry of God ringeth out, Whom shall I send, and who will go for us? And if so be that there respondeth a Person, and saith, Here am I, send me; and that one hath both the Impress of God upon the face of him, and a thick coating of Glue upon his purpose, then doth God arrive.

But God doth look often in his Stamp Box and find Whole Strips of Blank Margins. ✺

The Pulloon

Τhe daughter of the daughter of Keturah sat on the Curb, and she looked like a Small Sized Picture of Dejection. She lifted not her head when I drew near, and when I spake to her, she answered as it were in a Whisper that was nigh unto Tears. And she tried hard, and she could not Produce the Tears.

And I took her in my arms to comfort her.

And she laid her head against my shoulder, and her little warm face did she rub against my face. And she tried hard to cry.

And I said, Wherefore is my little maiden sad? And why hath her countenance fallen?

And she answered me with a Near-sob. And she said, We have no Money.

And I said, At the Present Price of almost everything, Money is not quite a Superfluity. Wherefore dost thou desire Money?

And she said, I desire a Pulloon.

And I understood her not. And I said, Speak not to me in that sobbing voice. What is that thou desirest? Is it a Prune?

And she told me that it was not a Prune.

And I asked her, What is a Pulloon like unto?

And she said, It is a Round Ball, of Red, or Blue, or Gold, and it Saileth High in the air, but it hath a String to Pull, lest it ascend to Heaven. Then understood I why she thought the name was Pulloon. For the name of a thing must have a meaning to her.

And I said, Come with me into the House, and let us see Baby Brother, and as for the Pulloon, forget it. I have not seen a man that selleth Pulloons in Many a Moon.

And we went into the house. And the daughter of Keturah laid her young son in mine arms, whom she hath named for me. And he is a Goodly Child.

And even as we stood there, behold I heard the sound of a whistle. And I caught the hand of the little maiden, and I said, Let us hasten. Behold there is such a thing as a Special Providence. And we hailed the seller of Pulloons. And he had Red ones and Blue ones and Green ones. And she was hard put to it to determine which she would take.

And the man watched her warily, for he knew what Grandfathers less wise than I did at such times. And he said,

One for Fifteen cents; two for a Quarter.

And I said, Pulloons have Gone up. Nevertheless, even if they were cheaper I would buy but one. For I know the folly of supposing that a child's life consisteth in the multitude of the Pulloons which she possesseth.

And we selected one. And the little maiden took it, and ran with it, and laughed, and it sailed above her Golden Curls; but her heart rose higher and danced more merrily than did the Pulloon. And mine heart went up with hers.

For we all sail our Pulloons. Yea, my heart is in the air with one of them, wherein rideth a Son of mine that saileth over the Ships to warn them of perils.

Yea, I have invested Rather Heavily in Pulloons.
Pulloons cost more than they did. ❧

The End
of the War

I and Keturah we go away in the Good Old Summertime, and we sojourn for Two Months beside a Little Lake. And there is a tree that groweth close down by the Lake whereon every year the Leaves turn Red at the beginning of the last week in August. Then know we that it is time to Pack our Baggage.

And on the first day of September in this present year did we return to our home. And our Daughter greeted us at the door. For she had come to set the house in order, and she brought with her the small Grandson who is named for me, and her little daughter also. And when the little damsel knew that we were there, for she was playing in the garden, then did she come running. And I went to meet her with my arms outstretched, and she also spread her arms so that all of her little pink fingers spread out. And her eyes were sparkling, and her Golden Hair was dancing as she came.

And these were the words wherewith she greeted me, saying,

O, Grandpa! Is the War over?

The little maiden hath a Service Flag, and it containeth Six Stars. For there be three brothers of her father in the Army, and three brothers of her mother, yea my sons and the sons of Keturah, in the Navy, including them that ride above the ships in what the little damsel doth call Pulloons. And her thought of absence and of homecoming was all of the war. Therefore did she inquire, saying, O, Grandpa! Is the War over?

Now there came a day when the War was over. And the bell rang in the Church; yea, with mine own hands did I ring it, while it was yet night. And the people thronged the streets so that all that day and far into the night the streets were Impassable for the Multitude. And I took the little maiden, and I carried her on my shoulder where the crowd was great, that she might see and remember all her life the wild tumult of them that cheered when Peace came again from Heaven upon Earth. And I mingled with the throng, and I rejoiced with them. And I saw the Mirth and the Rejoicing.

But when I think of the coming of Peace, there riseth before my mind the vision, not of the Crowd, neither of the sound of the Musick of the Bands, neither the Noise of them that blow Horns and Pound upon Pans, but the vision everywhere of Little Children who run, one by one, to meet returning soldiers, and cry in their Childish Joy, Is the War over?

And I thank God for the answer that shall be made unto them. ❧

The Minister
and the Saw

Now there came to me one of the sons of the Prophets, even a young minister, and he said, My church treateth me harshly.

And I said, What hast thou done to thy Church?

And he said, I upbraided them, and I told them they were Miserable Sinners.

And I answered, Thou didst speak truthfully and unwisely.

And he said, Is it not wise to speak the truth?

And I said, It is not wise to speak anything else; but Truth is precious, and should be used with Economy.

And he said, There were Great Reforms that needed to be wrought in that Town, and a Great Work to be done, and I had hoped to Inspire the Church to Do Those Things. But they are Stiff-necked, and they seek to Fire me.

And I said to him, Come with me into my Garden.

And we went out into the Garden, and I took with me a Saw.

And I said, Climb thou this tree, for thou art younger than I.

And he climbed the Tree, and sat upon a Limb thereof as I showed him.

And I said, That limb needeth to be Cut Off. Take thou the saw and Cut it Off.

And he began to saw beyond him.

And I said, Saw on the other side.

And he began to saw, but he stopped, and he said, If I saw the limb between myself and the Tree, I shall surely fall.

And I said unto him, The Minister who pusheth a Reform faster than his Church will follow, and findeth himself Fired, is like unto one who Ascendeth a Tree, and Saweth off a Limb between himself and the Tree.

And I left him there, and I went into mine House. And he sat there Some Little Time in Deep Meditation.

And he Climbed Down, and returned to his own Church. And he called the elders thereof together, and he said, I have been foolish, and have sought to Bring in the Millennium Before Sundown. Be patient with me, and I will strive to be more patient with the Church.

And they answered and said, Now thou art Talking like a man of Sense. Continue thou to chasten us for our sins, and show us how to be better, but expect not the Impossible, and lo, we will stand by thee till the Cows Come Home.

And the minister whom the Church was about to Fire took thought, and added a Cubit to his Stature; and his Church Rallied about him, and the last I heard some of the things he wanted to Get Done were being done.

And he wrote me a letter, saying,

O Safed, thou didst have me Up a Tree, but behold I am down and on the Job, and if thou wouldst see a happy and united and hustling Church, where the people love their minister, and the minister loveth his people, and where everything is up and moving, and good is being done, come over and see us.

And I read the letter and rejoiced. For there are Ministers who have learned How to Saw, but neither When nor Where. And if they will Climb my Apple Tree I will teach them wisdom. ❧

Heroes
and Heroines

There came to me a man and a woman, even an Husband and his Wedded Wife, and they said, We are weary one of the other.

And I said, Why is it thus?

And they said, We have grown commonplace to each other. Once we were to each other an Hero and an Heroine, but now we are Neither.

And I said, Napoleon did not look heroic to Josephine after she had seen him with his Suspenders hanging down his back; neither did Joan of Arc look heroic when she held her Front Hair in her mouth while she did up her back hair.

And they said, But he was an Hero and she was an Heroine.

And I said, Heroes and Heroines cannot appear heroic all the time. Caesar did not look heroic when he had pushed his slippers too far back under the bed, and he had to get down and fish them out with an umbrella; but that be a necessary thing, even to Heroes and Heroines.

And I said to the woman, When the Baby was sick, eight years ago, did not this thine Husband watch with thee day and night?

And she said, He did.

And I said unto the man, When thou hadst lost half thy money in a Fool Speculation, did she not stick by thee like a Little Burr, and cheer thee up, and never say, I told thee so?

And he said, It is even so.

And I said, Go down on your knees.

And they knelt.

And I said, Join hands.

And they did so.

And I prayed to God on their behalf, till there came to their eyes tears of Memory and Love.

And I Smote them lightly on the back, and I said, I dub thee an Hero; I dub thee an Heroine.

And I sent them forth.

And they lived happily ever afterward. ❧

The Bed
and the Mattress

I journeyed unto a distant City. And I made a Speech. And I tarried there until the next day.

And one of the principal citizens invited me unto his home. And I went with him, and he entreated me well.

Now when he had shown me unto my Room, I beheld that all the Furniture was of Solid Mahogany. And the Bedstead was a Work of Art. But when I laid my Weary Form upon the Bed, I sought to sleep, and I could not. For the Mattress also was of Solid Mahogany or something quite as Uncomfortable, and with Knots in the Mahogany. And the Spring sagged, so that it deposited me in an Heap in the middle of the Bed, and I required a Derrick wherewith to get out of it.

Now the good God, who made the Trees, made them of many kinds, and the Wood of those trees hath each of them its own variety of Beauty. And I love the color of Mahogany, even when I suspect that it is Birch with a Stain upon it. But when I go unto my Bed, I soon forget the color of the wood, and I desire a Good Mattress and a Comfortable Spring.

And I considered concerning mine Hospitable Hosts that they had had about Fifty Dollars wherewith to buy a

Bedstead and Spring and Bed for their Guest Room, and they had spent Forty of it for the Bedstead, and divided the Ten which they had left between a Sagging Spring and a Solid Mahogany Mattress with Lumps in It.

Now I considered that there are other people who do likewise. For I went unto the House of God, and there rose a Preacher, and he Preached. But he had put Forty Dollars of his Preparation into the Framework of his Sermon, and had only Ten Dollars and Five Minutes left wherein to Preach the Gospel.

And I called upon a man who was not a preacher, and I found that he was putting Forty Dollars of his Energy into Getting a Living, and less than ten dollars into the actual business of Living.

And I thought about the Solid Mahogany Bed and Mattress, and I said, The people who read these Parables are High Brow, and they want no Parables made out of such Homely and Commonplace Things. But I opened the book of the Prophet Isaiah, and I found there the words that he said,

The bed is shorter than that a man can stretch himself upon it, and the covering narrower than that he can wrap himself in it.

And I knew that Isaiah was a tall man, even as I, and that when the bedclothes pulled out at the foot, he could make a Parable out of it for the High-brow people of Jerusalem. And I thought I would take a chance at it.

For there are many people in life who put too much into the Mahogany Bedstead and not enough into the Mattress and the Spring. ❧

Decorations and the Unexpected Wedding

There was to be a Wedding at Eight of the clock. And the Bride's Family had gotten things up Regardless. For it was their Only and Beloved Daughter who was to be Married, and they loved her. And they spent a Lot of Money on Decorations. And the Altar of God was a Bower of Roses within the Temple.

And about Four of the clock, the Preparation was all Finished. And the Decorator and his Assistants went their way. But the Organist was practicing for the evening.

And there drave up a Brand New Automobile, and two folk emerged and said, We desire to be Married. And they produced a Marriage License on which the Ink was Hardly Dry.

And the man said unto me, Fear not the newness of it. It is all right. We live in a city an hundred miles from here, and I am a Dealer in Automobiles. And I come hither when I have a New Car to take home, and I drive it home from here, and save freight. And we have long known each other and have determined to be married; and last night I had a wire that a new car was in the City for me, and we came on the train to the City, and I got my Car and my License, and when we are married, we shall go on our way Rejoicing.

And I went with them into the Temple, and I spake unto the organist, and he Practiced the Wedding March for them to come in, and I married them before the Decorated Altar.

And as they left, he said, I have heard much of thee, that thou art a Famous man and that thou treatest folk well who come unto thee, but I never expected Anything Like This.

And they went away happy.

And four hours later the Big Wedding came, with the White Kid Gloves, and the Flower Girls and the Many Maids and Ushers, and the Decorations showed not one wilted petal on account of the joy which they had already given to another couple.

Now I considered this matter, and I looked about in the world, and considered how many Plant Flowers in their Front Yards, which cost me no Labour, but which I do enjoy; and I feel like going up to their Door, and ringing their Bell and thanking them. And I considered how God made this World a Long Time Ago, and did most of the Decoration for Other Folk, at least in part. But I find myself here, with the Decorations and the Musick and I am Sufficiently Wise to Go Down the Aisle of my Mortal Pilgrimage with a Glad Smile, both for that which hath been Specially Prepared for me and for the good things which I share with others. And I hope to leave the situation not one particle the worse for those who are to tread the Aisle after me. ✌

The Unopened
Window

Now there came to me a man with a Sad Countenance, and he said, O Safed, thy words of wisdom are known to all, and thy virtue exceedeth even thy wisdom; may thy days be long.

And I heard him, and I answered not; for the one who cometh unto me with a Little Too Much Taffy and Then Some hath an Axe to Grind. And I said, If thou hast Business, say on; for Time Passeth.

And he said, O Safed, I have a neighbor, and he is an Undesirable Citizen. His house joineth hard unto mine upon the North, and he annoyeth me continually. He and his Kids keep up a continual Rough House, which greatly annoyeth us. And he hath Daughters, and there come to see them Young Men, who sit with them on the Porch till Any Old Time at Night, and they Laugh and Raise Ned so that sleep is driven from our eyes, and slumber from our eyelids. Yea, and when we look that way we see things that Vex our Righteous Souls.

And I said, Are they Immoral? If so thou mayest call the Police.

And he said, They are not what you might call Immoral, for my wife hath watched them much through the

Window; she hath a place where she sitteth and watcheth while she Darneth Stockings; yet are they noisy; yea, they are the Limit.

And I said unto him, How many windows hath thy house?

And he said, My house standeth Foursquare, and it hath windows toward the North, the South, the East and the West.

And I said unto him, Move thou over to the South side of thy House; thou shalt have more Sleep and Sunshine. Yea, moreover, speak thou unto thy wife that she Darn her Stockings where she hath less to see.

And he went away angry.

But I counted it among my Good Deeds.

And I meditated thereon, and I considered that there are many people who live on the North Side of their own Souls; yea, they curse God that they hear the racket and are sad; and behold, their South Windows are unopened. ℘

The Chickens
and the Mush

Now Keturah considered the High Cost of Living, and she said, Let us buy an Incubator, and keep Hens. So she sold her Waste Paper to the Rag Man, and she bought an incubator, and put Eggs therein, and in thrice seven days the Eggs Hatched, and there came forth Little Chickens. And Keturah fed them.

And it came to pass on a day that I went into the yard, and beheld Keturah feeding the Chickens. And that whereon she fed them was Mush.

And she took the Mush from a Bowl with a Spoon, and she dropped a great Spoonful on the Ground. And all the Little Chickens ran every one of them after the Mush.

And she walked on a little farther and dropped another Spoonful. And all the little chickens forsook the first Spoonful and ran after the second. Yea, they trod every one of them upon the Mush which they had been eating that they might Hasten after other Mush.

And she went on a little farther and dropped a third Spoonful. And all the little chickens forsook the second Spoonful and ran after the third. And the Mush of the first Spoonful and of the second Spoonful they despised.

And some of the chickens got none of any of the three

Spoonfuls. But if part of them had gone to each Spoonful they might all have had Mush. Nevertheless, did they all follow Keturah all around the Lot, and every chicken was Among Those Present when the last Spoonful was dropped.

And I meditated much thereon. And I said, Keturah, Men are like Chickens.

And Keturah said, What about Women?

And I said, No matter how good is the food they already have, yet do they forsake it and run where the last Fad droppeth. And what they obtain after all their running is but Mush.

And I spake again, and I said, Keturah, Men are like unto young chickens.

And Keturah said, So are Women. ❧

The Seven Targets

Now in the City where I dwelt were divers Shooting Galleries, and some of them charge Five Cents for Three Shots, and there were others that Gave Five Shots for Five Cents. And I Noticed when I passed their gates, and if the Sign Read Three Shots for Five Cents, I entered Not; but if it Read Five Shots for Five Cents, then I entered.

And one of the Galleries where I went had Seven Targets, all in One Row. And the Targets had each of them a Bullseye. And the Targets were each of the Same Size, about a Cubit in breadth; but the Bullseyes were Divers. For the one on the Right hand had a Bullseye as small as the Fingernail of a man's Hand, and the one on the left had a Bullseye as large as a Silver Dollar, and those that were between Grew as the Targets were placed from the Right side to the left. And there were on each Target Rings round the Bullseye, from the Bullseye to the Outer Edge of the Target. And he who Hit the Bullseye on any Target whatsoever caused a Bell to Ring.

Now, in my youth I could Shoot Some, and in my Riper Years I Can Shoot a Little. So it was my custom to Choose a Target near the Middle, and Sometimes I made the Bell to Ring, perhaps twice or thrice out of Five.

But it came to pass on a day that I entered a Gallery, and laid down a silver Coin which was the Fourth Part of a Dollar, and the Man gave me Four Nickels and a Gun. And I took the Gun, and I said, I have not practiced of late; I will take the Large Bullseye. So I shot, and I Hit It. And I shot again, and I Hit it Again. And thus I did Five Times.

And it Pleased me that I had Hit the Bullseye and Rung the Bell Five times.

And I handed the Man another Nickel, and I Hit the Bullseye Five Times More. And I was yet more pleased.

And I gave him Another Nickel, and Yet another Five Times I Did the Same.

And I said within my heart, Behold, am not I a good Shot?

And I gave him Another Nickel.

And the Man took the Nickel, and gave me Another Gun, for I had shot out all that the First Gun contained; moreover, it needed Cleaning, by reason of the Shooting I had done. Now the man who kept the Gallery Had been regarding me, and I thought he had been Admiring my Skill, but he had Not. For when he had handed me the Second Gun, and taken my Fourth Nickel he spake to me thus:

Now if all you want is to Hear Yourself Ring the Big Bell, you can Probably Continue to Do That for a Considerable Time to Come; but if you really want to Improve Your Shooting, you will never shoot at anything but the Smallest Bullseye. You will put your shots into quite as Small a Circle, and you will have the Advantage of Knowing Just How Much you lack of Being a Really Good Shot.

And the word went to my heart.

So I walked to the other end, and I shot five times at the Small Bullseye, and I hit it Not Once. But all my Shots were close in, and every one of them would have Rung the Big Bell. So I gave him my Last Nickel, and I Shot Five times more and out of the Five Shots I Rang the Small Bell Twice.

And though it sounded not so loud as the Big Bell, yet I knew in my heart it was Better Shooting, and that it had Compelled me to do My Best.

Then I said in my heart, O my God, I have lived an Upright Life among my Neighbors, and often have they Told me So; but I fear lest I have been Shooting at the Big Bell. Mine have not been the Cruel Temptations of Some Others, yet I have Had Pride that I was better than Some of them. O my God, I will seek henceforth to Shoot at the Smallest Target. Then shall I know how much I lack of being really a Good Shot.

And I told the Parable to some of my Neighbors, and I said, Behold, I went in to the House of Shooting, and I heard a sermon that divided between the joints and marrow of my soul. And they, too, were humbled when they heard it. ❧

The Private Car

There is a certain man whose abiding place is a city where is a great Railway Station, even a Terminal, and this man determined within himself that he would go upon a Journey. So he walked unto the Terminal, and he bought a Ticket, and he paid the Fare. And he presented the Ticket at a Gate where stood a Watchman and the Watchman punched his Ticket and spake unto him saying, Thy train is all ready on Track Number Six.

And he beheld the Cars, and they were filling up rapidly. And he said, Behold, they will all be crowded, and I shall suffer Discomfort.

And he beheld the last Car, which was nearest unto the Gate, and behold, there was no one in it. And he said,

This will I do. I will go into that Car, and I shall have Abundant Room.

So he went within, and he had all the Room he Wanted, even the Whole Car. And he smiled within himself when he thought of the other Passengers who were Jammed into the other Cars.

And while he was Hugging Himself for Joy, and considering what a smart Guy he was, behold, the train pulled out, and left him and his Private Car standing upon the track.

And he rushed out and spake angrily unto the Watchman, and he said, Wherefore am I left behind?

And the Watchman said, That is an Extra Car which we keep on the track to use in case there be a greater crowd than we expect, but today there was no great crowd. Yea, and there had been room enough for thee in one of the cars that went, but thou didst want more room, and thou hast all the room in sight. Yea, and upon the Side Track out in the yard are many empty cars. Thou canst take thy seat in any one of them. But if thou desirest to ride unto the City for which thy Ticket readeth, behold there will be another train in four hours and fifteen minutes; and take heed that thou enter the cars that go.

Now, this I beheld, for I was in the Station, even the Terminal, and I saw that man, yea, and I heard that man: and what I heard was a plenty.

And I considered that often I am caught in the Jam of life, with people crowding and pushing, and it were much more comfortable to find a quiet seat in some Rear Car, where the wicked cease from troubling and the weary are at rest. But I considered how that if one is to get anywhere he must go with Folks, even though they crowd, and that no one can do very much without the companionship and help of others. Therefore did I resolve to keep out of the Private Cars that do not go. For I have seen that for the lack of the ability to do this, some are left on the track in their own Private Car, while the enterprises of life move on. ❧

The Points
of the Compass

Once upon a time I journeyed unto a great city whose name was New York. And I lodged in an Inn other than that wherein I had lodged previously. And when I arose in the morning I was Turned Around. For the North appeared unto me to be West and East appeared North. And I could not make it seem right, albeit I knew which way to go; for I had been there before.

And I went unto Twenty-third Street and stood looking toward the place where Fifth Avenue doth Gee toward the right hand and Broadway Haweth to the left. And then I recalled the vision of the town where I was born.

And straight before me I saw the little White Church, and I knew that I was looking North. And on my right down Twenty-third Street I saw the Red Brick School House, and I knew that it was East, and behind me I knew was the Town Hall. And on my left hand I saw the house where I was born, over against the Town Pump, on Main Street where it joineth unto Richmond Street.

Thus did I pick up the city of New York and set it upon the top of a Flat Iron Building, and twist it around till the points of its compass agreed with those of the town where I was born. And I was Turned Around no more.

And this same stunt have I wrought in London and Los Angeles, and in Paris and Pittsburg; I have done it in New Orleans and I shall do it if there is occasion in the New Jerusalem, which standeth four square.

And this also have I done in Matters of Morals. For I learned other things than the points of the Compass in the little town wherein I was born. I learned the Ten Commandments, and the Golden Rule, and divers other good things. I learned Invaluable Things in the Red Brick School House that is turned toward the rising of the sun, and in the Church that is toward the North Star, and in the house that stood over against the Town Pump, where Main Street joineth unto Richmond Street. And when I am perplexed concerning great matters of right and wrong, I pick up the Great Problems of Political Economy and International Law, and Corporate Responsibility, and I resolve the whole matter upon the Town Pump of the place where I was born, until I find how its Moral Directions conform to the points of the Compass in Ethicks which I learned from Godly Parents, and faithful though not brilliant pastors, and competent though not Illustrious Teachers.

Now there be those who Consider that this process is Provincial, and who think themselves Very Clever for having outgrown this method. But the Compass pointeth Straight toward the North Star in the room where I knelt by my Mother's Knee; and out of the window in the morning I did Ever behold the Rising Sun, and it rose ever in the East. ❧

The Moving
Pictures

We took a journey, I and Keturah, and we Changed Cars in a certain city, and we lodged there One Night in an Inn. And we walked abroad after that we had Dined, and it was evening. And the Shops were closed, but the Movies were open. And we gave Two Dimes unto a Damsel in a Glass Cage, and we went in and sat down.

And we beheld a Moving Picture, the theme whereof was The Reward of Virtue. And it was concerning a Young Woman who loved Art with a Capital A, and who appeared not to love Dishwashing. And she left her Home and went to a Great City and Studied Art. And she was subject to Great Temptations, all of which were Shown to us, and the way she was Tempted was A Plenty. But nothing tempted her to go Back Home and help her mother Wash the Dishes in the Kitchen Sink. So she Came to the Very Brink. And the man who Tempted her Most was a Millionaire in Disguise. And the More he Tempted her the more he Loved her. And when he found that he could not have her without Marrying her, he offered to marry her. And they were Married. So the Reward of Virtue was Cash in the Bank. And we Sat Through this Highly Moral Movie. And we yawned, both of us.

Then spake I to Keturah, and said, There are Two More Films. Shall we stay for them?

And she said, This stuff doth not amuse me.

And I said, It is not up to Our Speed. Let us go.

So we went while the Going was Good.

And as we wandered, we came to a Down Town Church, where the rich had moved away, and the poor remained. And the door was open and we went in. And there was a Prayer Meeting. And there were Not as Many people there as there were at the Movies. And they who loved the Lord spake there to each other, and comforted one another, and lifted their prayers to God for Courage for the Day's Job.

And we saw in their Faces, and heard in their Words such Dramas and Tragedies as No Movie ever invented. And the Reward of Virtue for them was in Faith to go on, and the Approval of Conscience, and the Peace of God.

And we Returned unto the Inn, and I answered Keturah, and said,

That also was a Moving Picture, and it was Great Stuff.

And Keturah said, That was the Real Thing. That was Life.

And when we knelt beside our Bed that Night, we Prayed for Both Companies of People. ❧

The Ancient Train

It came to pass that I was upon a journey, and I lodged in a certain City, and I arose early in the morning to go forward upon my journey. And the Train came in on time, and I got on board. And it was not the kind of Train which I expected. For the Train that was advertised was an Express Train, with Pullman Cars and other Expensive Luxuries, and this Train had no such things. For there was only an Engine, and a Baggage Car and one Coach. And the Coach was a Very Old One.

And the Passengers began to make Remarks. And one said, that this Coach had descended from Mount Ararat, and that there had been no Improvements made upon it since Noah used it as an Ark. And many such like things did they say.

But I spake unto myself, saying, There is a Reason, and if we be Patient, we shall discover it.

And the Conductor came through. And he wore no Uniform; but had a Badge on an Elastick Band, fastened around a Derby Hat. And I had not seen the like in many years.

And the Passengers made Remarks to him about the kind of Train on which we were riding.

And he answered not a word, until he had taken up all his Tickets. Then he stood in the Aisle and delivered an Oration. And he said:

I have listened to the Fool Remarks of you who think you are Wise concerning the quality of this Train. Be it understood by all of you that this is not the Regular Train, neither am I the Conductor of that Train. But I got out of bed at Four A.M. to run this Flivver from the Junction to the Terminal as an accommodation to you who have not sense enough to suspect that somebody is trying to do you a Favor. For it was known to us that about Twenty Passengers were arriving at the Junction, and others to be picked up here, and we wanted to help you out. And because our regular crews are overworked, and many of our men are sick with Flu, it was no easy job to get an Engineer and a Switch Engine and a couple of old Cars. And because there was no Conductor available, therefore did the Division Manager undertake to see this Train to its Destination, and that's me. And I was able to get away and take this Train, because I have to go to the Terminal this morning; and I was minded to take the Switch Engine and go, but I made up this Train for your sakes. And now, if any of you want the Limited, and are discontented with the Train, behold, I will stop this old boat, and let you out, and ye can walk back or wait for it just as ye prefer. For the Limited is in the Ditch about Fifty Miles back, and the track behind us will be blocked until Noon.

And no one decided to get off and walk, neither did any complain more of our Train.

And I considered this thing, and I said, that if we were to stop and think before complaining, we should sometimes discover that the things whereof we complain are those for which we should be Thankful. ❧

The Piece Cut Out of the Paper

There is a way that I have learned whereby I may fool Keturah; and because there be so few things in which I can fool her, and so many in which I should like to do so, and because there be few who know even one such way, therefore do I record it.

There cometh to our door every morning a lad who bringeth unto us a Daily Paper; save that on the Sabbath he bringeth it not. For on that day do I desire to have rest from some of the things of the week. And there cometh to our door twice every day a Postman, and he bringeth many other papers. And I read them with Shears, so that when I read something that I would read again, then do I cut it out.

And Keturah hath no more than her share of Curiosity, yet is there nothing which she hath so keen a desire to know as what was in the Piece that I have Cut Out. And sometimes she careth for nothing else in the Paper, but she fain would know what was the Article which I have cut out.

Therefore have I learned this, that when I would cut out an Article, I will cut out the Whole Page. And from the page do I clip out the Piece that I want, and throw the rest into the Wastebasket. Then doth Keturah read the paper and Miss Nothing. So do I keep Peace with her, and save the Piece that I cut out. For even though she misseth a page, and therewith the end of an article, yet doth it not offend her like the cutting out of a Little Square from the middle of the page.

Now I have considered this, and I have reflected that it is often possible to do a Large Thing and get away with it, whereas a Small Thing of the like kind doth only irritate.

Forlorn Hopes

There came unto me a man, who saluted me and sat down. And he was of a sorrowful countenance.

And he said, O Safed, thou great and wise man, live forever.

And I said, Eliminate that Stuff, and say what it is that devoureth thee: for I behold that thou art in trouble.

And he said, Thy servant is a Publick Spirited Citizen in the town where he doth reside, and he is chairman of many Committees for the doing of what all agree ought to be done and none desireth to do. And behold, there is a great undertaking which hath been begun, and all interest in it hath slumped and our Great Cause is now a Forlorn Hope. And only a Miracle can save it.

And I said, Then let there be a Miracle.

And he said, Thou speakest as if Miracles were Dead Easy.

And I answered, They are not easy, but they are sometimes necessary. And the most miraculous of Miracles is the resurrection of Forlorn Hopes; but Most Successful Achievements are of that sort.

And I said, Hast thou heard of the Pilgrims?

And he said, I have known of them all my life.

And I said, Six weeks before the Pilgrims left Holland their adventure was a Forlorn Hope. In the year of our Lord one thousand six hundred and twenty, and on the sixth month and the fourteenth day of the month, John Robinson, that man of God, wrote that there were none among the Pilgrims who would then put money into the Enterprise if he had back what already he had put in.

And he said, I never knew that. I supposed that all those Old Saints were sustained throughout by their Faith in God, and their visions of the Glorious Future.

And I said, It is the habit of God to get us committed to tasks greater than we can achieve and see whether we be cowardly or brave. For no one ever prayeth save when he faceth Something Bigger than he can do alone. But when a person doth realize that he and God must see it through together, or else give up and quit, then doth that person Pray Mightily and go forward, and the sea doth open, or the Jordan divide, or mountains remove and become an Highway.

And I said, The statue erected some time ago to the memory of Lot's wife, standeth in Comparative Isolation; but if every person who had faltered and thought the cause a Forlorn Hope had given it up, then were there no Salt left in the Dead Sea.

And he said, I think I understand.

And I said, Go thou home, and seek the blessing of God anew, and add one more to the long list of Forlorn Hopes that became Glorious Achievements. ❧

The
Laundry

The Waggon from the Laundry stopped at the door, and
left a Package. And Keturah opened it, and checked up the
Contents. And she said, Two of thy Collars are missing, and
one Cuff; and thy Pajamas have lost a sleeve.

And I went unto the Telephone, and I said unto the
Maiden at the Laundry, I beseech of thee, send unto me the
missing portions of my attire.

And she said unto me, Our manager is out; thou wilt
have to see him.

And I went to the Laundry, and I entered it as the
Manager entered. And I had in mind to say unto him that
his service had grown Intolerable, and that he no longer
cleaned Collars but Sharpened them and put Saw Teeth
upon the edges of them, and that what Clothes he did not
lose, he ruined.

And as the Manager entered, there came unto him one
of his Assistants, who said unto him, The man at the factory
saith that he cannot put in that Crank-shaft for Two Weeks.

And his Bookkeeper said unto him, The Driver of
Number Three hath quit, for he had an opportunity to

become a Chauffeur for Old Jones who liveth on the Boulevard; and how shall we deliver the laundry on his run?

And the Forewoman in the Ironing Room said unto him, Saidee is home sick, and Fanny hath gone to the Movies, and Kitty hath sent word that she must attend her Grandmother's funeral, which is probably the Foot-ball Game; and two of the Machines in my room are shut down, and the people are kicking because they have not their clothes.

And the Telephone Girl said, We have complaints from the Families whose names and number I have here, and they desire that thou Call them Up and explain.

And he said, I will call them up, but it shall be some time in the Very Remote Future; I have troubles enough.

And other of his assistants told him that they were nearly out of Soap, and that the people who sold Starch had sent word that they could not fill the order for ten days.

And the Manager greeted me with a Tired Look, as if he were to say, And what hast thou brought to add to my Troubles?

And I said unto him, I came to Complain of certain Lost Garments, but I forbear.

And he said pleasantly, Nevertheless, let me know thy Complaint, and we will endeavor to make it Right.

And we went to the Sorting Room, and I saw how the Girls sorted the Laundry, and I thought if anyone did ever get what was coming to him, it would have been by Special Providence. And there was a Pile of Arms from shirts, and Legs from other garments, and many things besides. And I found the Arm of my Pajamas.

And I returned unto Keturah, and I said, I will complain no more concerning the man of the Laundry. He hath Troubles enough, and I wonder that he doeth as well as he doth.

And I considered that it might be the same if I knew more of the affairs of others concerning whom I have been impatient. And it may be that if they could look into the place in which I endeavor to do my part in Cleaning up the World, they would be more patient with me. ✺

Concerning
Vacations

Now I dwelt in a city and the labor of the weeks was heavy, so it came to pass as Summer Approached, that every year I went on a Vacation. And ofttimes I rode upon a Stage in the hills of Vermont, the Driver whereof was a man of experience. And he spake to me ofttimes, and every year this was the burden of his complaint:

Behold, thou comest here again on thy vacation, being a man who toilest not, nor spinnest, nor gatherest into barns, and the Greater Part of those who ride on my Stage in the Good Old Summer Time come Likewise; but I drive this Condemned Old Stage Year in and Year out, Wet or Dry, Hot or Cold, and for Forty Years I have had no Vacation.

Now when I had heard this many times, I wrote to the Manager of the Stage Route, saying:

Behold this Driver of thy Company hath served long, and hath never had a Vacation; give him Two Weeks, that he may have a Vacation like unto the Rest of Humankind.

And they did as I made request of them, and they sent Another Driver to Drive the Stage for Two Weeks, that he might have a Vacation.

CONCERNING VACATIONS

And the Next Summer as I came that way, I asked him concerning his Vacation, and where and how he had Spent it.

And he relieved himself of a burden he had been carrying, namely, a mouthful of Tobacco Juice, and thus he made answer:

The first Day, being Monday, I rode with the New Driver to show him the Road; and because he was slow to Learn I rode with him also on Tuesday. And on Wednesday I feared lest the Bay Mare should have cast a Shoe, and I rode with him again, and stopped at the Blacksmith Shop in the place midway, for there dwelleth the only Smith who knoweth how to Shoe Horses as they ought to be shod. And on Thursday Widow Skiles was going to Town, and I knew her Trunk must go, and I feared lest that Substitute Driver should have forgotten it. And on Friday it looked as if it would Rain, and was no kind of Day for a person to be starting on his Vacation, so I rode on the stage that Day also. And on Saturday it did Rain, and was no kind of Day for a person to be sitting around inside the House with Nothing to Do, so I rode again that day. And on Monday there were a lot of City Folks who had been out in the Hills for the Week-End, going back to the City, and some of them were a Leetle Mite p'tic'lar, and I thought I might as well Go Long, and see them git on the Train. And Tuesday I realized that the Time was more'n Half Gone, and a Feller couldn't do Nothing in One Week Nohow, so I just continnered to Ride on the Stage with the Substitute Driver, and Show him How. And by the End of the Second Week he was a Pretty Good Driver, and if I could have had a Vacation then, I could have trusted him to run the Stage.

Thus spake to me the Driver, who had always complained that he had never had a Vacation.

And I meditated much concerning what he had said to me.

And I said, O my God, let me not be one of those who constantly complain of the blessings they do not have, and who Would not Know What to Do with them if they had them. ❧

Two
Shadows

Now it came to pass in the Summer that I sojourned by the side of a Little Lake that lay to the westward of my habitation. And there was an evening when I watched the Sun as it was going down, and behold it was Glorious. And as I turned away from it and entered my dwelling, behold mine own Shadow went before me, and climbed up upon the inner wall of the Room as I entered. And as I went forward, lo, another Shadow rose upon the wall, and it was like unto the first, even mine own Shadow. And I marveled much that one man should cast Two Shadows. And the Thing Seemed Passing Strange.

But the reason was this, that the Sun as it was going down shone on the water and was like unto another Sun, and cast a Shadow even brighter and taller than the Sun in the heavens. For the Sun in the heavens was partly obscured by the trees; but the Sun in the lake cast its reflected rays under the branches and shone clearly. And so it was that in my sight the reflected Sun was brighter than the real Sun, and cast the greater and taller Shadow.

And I thought within my soul how to the men and women the vision of the Most High God is often obscured; and how there be those who must see the exceeding brightness of His Person by reflected light. And I prayed to my God that such light of Him as I may reflect might reveal to such as behold it the true glory of the Sun of Righteousness. ✤

The Sunset
That Followed Us

There came for me an Automobile, that it might convey me unto another City, where they desired me to speak upon an Afternoon. And the daughter of the daughter of Keturah desired that she might go with me.

And I said, Let her go. There will be a long ride, and a long program; but we shall have a good time.

And when her mother consented, then did the little maiden weep. For she said, I want to go, but it is Very Far and Very Long.

And I said, Weep not. Thus doth thy Grandmother ever when a Good Thing cometh her way, and she considereth whether it will cost a Dollar that she might give to the Poor, or cause her to be absent from a Missionary Meeting.

And we had a Great Ride for an hundred and three score furlongs. And when we arrived in the place of Assembly, then the little maiden sat on the Front Seat among people whom she had never seen before and looked up at her Grandfather and was not afraid.

And we drove back as the sun went down, and she watched the Sunset out of the back window of the Car, and she said, See, Grandpa, the Sunset is following us; it is just a Mile Behind us.

Now on that day she had learned how far a Mile is, for I had showed her certain Barns and Houses and other things that were a Mile away. Therefore did she know how far away the Sunset was.

And she said, The Sun is going to sleep, but see how beautiful it is.

And it was even so. For as the Sun grew more sleepy, it smiled as its eyelids drooped, and the West was very Beautiful with the Happy Farewell of the Sleepy Sun. And the little maiden thought she had never seen anything so wonderful.

So we came again unto our home as the night came on, and the little maiden was so weary she could hardly open her mouth to eat her Bread and Milk before she went to Bed; and she scarce touched the Pillow till she was fast asleep.

And I thought of the Adventures of faith that our Heavenly Father doth invite us to undertake, and how far they seem and how perilous so that we weep even while we desire them. For so do folk at Weddings and at the other solemn and wonderful experiences of life. But there is a blessing that followeth all the way, and is never so much as a Mile Distant. ❧

The
First Robin

Now the Winter had been Long, and Very Cold, and the Snow had been deep, and Spring was not yet come. And I rose early in the morning, and I looked out of mine Window, and Behold a Robin.

And I called unto Keturah, and said, Come quickly, and see thou hasten thine arrival at the Window. For here is a Friend of ours that is Come from a Far Country to Visit us.

And Keturah came to the Window, and she also beheld the Robin.

Now the Robin looked at us, and hopped about upon the Cold and Bare Ground, and looked for the Early Worm, but the Bird was Earlier than the Worm. And Keturah went to her Kitchen to see what she might find that the Robin would eat.

And I spake to the Robin, and said:

Behold thou hast been where it was Warm, and the Sun did Shine. And thou couldest have stayed there. But here thou art. And thou comest while it is yet Winter, for the Prophecy of Spring is in thy Blood. Thy faith is the substance of things hoped for and the evidence of things not seen. Thou hast come many miles, yea hundreds of miles, to a land that lies desolate, because thou hast within thy soul the assurance that Spring is near. Oh, that there were in human life some assurance that would send folk forth to their High Destiny with as compelling a Conviction!

And I thought of the Eye, that it is formed in darkness, but formed for the light; and the Ear that is wondrously shaped in Silence, but made for the hearing of Musick; and of the Human Soul that is born into a world where Sin is, yet born with the hope of Righteousness.

And I blessed the Little Bird that had caused me to think of these things.

And I went forth into town that day, and people said, Safed. Behold is it not a cold and long Winter?

And I said, Speak to me no more of Winter.

And they said, Wherefore should we not speak of Winter? Behold the Thermometer and the Empty Coal Bin.

But I held mine Head Proudly and I said:

Speak to me not of Winter. Behold, on this morning I did see the First Robin. For me henceforth it is Spring.

The Home
of the Sparrow

There is a Great City, and there runneth a Street through the midst thereof, and on this side of the Street and on that are High Buildings. And some of them are like unto the Tower of Babel. And one of those buildings is named for the man who Discovered America. And upon the front of the building, even above the Main Entrance, and High above the Sidewalk, is a Graven Image of Christopher Columbus.

And I sat in that Building, beside a Window that looketh out as if Christopher Columbus had stepped through it to where his Image standeth.

And it was Winter. And the wind was Cold, and the snow Blew down the Street.

And under the garment of Christopher Columbus, and hard by one of his legs, was a Sparrow. And he had found for himself a place About as Snug and Comfortable as any bird could find out of doors on That Kind of a day. And he was sheltered from the Wind and from the Snow.

And the Sparrow was nigh unto the Window, so that I might almost have put forth my hand and taken him inside, but he was better off where he was. And the Sparrow saw me, and I saw the Sparrow, and we looked long at each other, and neither of us was afraid of the other.

And the Sparrow said within his heart, It is for Me that this building hath been erected, and this Statue lifted high, with this cozy place for a Shelter from the Storm. To this end did Christopher Columbus cross the Ocean, that he might have this Building named for him, and that I might have shelter.

Now when the bird spake thus in his heart, and I saw and understood the intent thereof, I did not chide the Sparrow, for I myself have had Just as Little Thoughts of the Providence of God and the Answer of my Prayers as the Sparrow. And while it was all Very Foolish, I am not so sure that it was as Foolish as it would have been to Stay out in the Storm till the Sparrow had learned For What Other Purpose Christopher Columbus crossed the Ocean, or for me to question too curiously What Larger Meaning there may be in the Providence of God.

Then said I, Oh, my God, I am of more value than many Sparrows, but I do not know much more than they, and some people know less. The Sparrow hath found her an House, and the Swallow a Nest in the Protecting Shelter of Thine Altars, and they know not that those Altars have any Other use. I do not know much more about thy Providences than that Sparrow knoweth about Christopher Columbus, but I know that when the Blast of the Terrible One is as a Storm Against the Wall, Thou dost keep him in Perfect Peace whose mind is stayed on Thee. ❧

The Nest
in the Spout

The Sparrow hath found her an house and the Swallow a nest in the House of God that standeth hard by to where I and Keturah we live, and the Pigeons also, they dwell there, and prosper and are happy.

Now in the summer time, when Rains are infrequent, they make their nests in every Old Place imaginable, and lay their eggs and hatch their young. And there is a window high up that overlooketh a place where a Gable projecteth, and there is an Eavespout and a Downspout. And the Downspout hath an Iron Grating over the top inside the Eavespout. And a Pigeon builded her nest above that grating. And it was a cool and well-ventilated nest.

And I and Keturah we saw it, and we said, That Pigeon taketh large chances.

But the Latter Rains delayed, and the little birds hatched, and they lay there shockingly Nude on top of the few sticks of a nest that were on the top of the grating in the Eavespout. And the Mother Pigeon brought them food, and I began to think that they would grow and get away before the Rains came and the storms blew.

But there came a night when there was a Storm.

And I wakened and Keturah wakened also.

And I knew what was in the mind of Keturah.

And I said, It is Foolish of us to be troubled about it. There are Pigeons enough, and they increase until they be a Nuisance. Nevertheless, I am not happy to think of them in that Place.

And I rose, and I went into the House of God. And the tempest was beginning to break, and the lightning flashed.

And I stretched forth my hand, and took the Frightened Little Things, and I brought them inside. And I carried them out, and placed them in a sheltered corner on the ground under where the nest had been. And the Mother Pigeon found them there and sheltered them till the storm was past.

Now that did not hurt me, nor greatly interrupt my sleep. For though I was wetted in the rain, yet Keturah had my Bath-Towel ready, and I was soon dry, and I went to sleep sooner than I should have done if I had thought of those little birds drowning in the cold rain.

And I said unto myself, It is not that the Pigeons are worth it, if one were to value his time and his labor; but there are other measures of value than those that may be estimated in cash.

And I said, I will never deny that in the sight of God we are Worth Saving. ❦

The
Crow

In the place where we go in the Summer, there cometh no Garbage-Man unto our Back Gate, but we take the Garbage unto a place remote from the house, and dump it in the Woods. Now my little Grandson went to empty out the Garbage, and he ran unto me saying, There is a Great Black Bird that is amid the Garbage, and he flieth not away. Howbeit, he stretcheth forth his Broad Wings as if he would Fly, but he flieth not.

And I went unto the place, and found a Crow; and it was even as he said. The Crow sought to fly but could not.

And I laid hold upon him, and I found that he had caught himself in a Briar. And the Long Thorns had entered his flesh in such fashion that when he sought to Fly the Green Briar tightened about him and the thorns went deeper into his flesh. And no man could have devised a Trap that thus would have caught a Crow, but that Crow was caught.

And I held him while I drew out the thorns, and there were but two of them, but they went deep into him. And when he was free from the Thorns, I considered.

And I took him unto Keturah, and the children they

also went with me. And I said, Any farmer would tell me what to do with this Crow. Shall I do as they tell me?

And Keturah said, Whatever a Farmer may do and ought to do concerning Crows that eat his corn, he may determine and not we. But this poor, wounded thing hath done us no harm, and the more Garbage he eateth the better. Let the children stroke his back for a little space, and then release him.

And this I did, and the Crow remained near us for certain days while his wounds healed, and he found his food in the same place where we found him. And I said, Elijah had his bread brought unto him by birds like unto you; credit this to Elijah on account.

And as I saw the Crow from day to day, I considered how content he was not to rob cornfields when other food was furnished unto him, and I wondered how many darkened lives have been made predatory because there was no way found to feed them from that which would have cost others little. For it is not the fault of the Crow, as I suppose, that he hath no red breast like the Robin, or beautiful song like the Nightingale.

Now this I know, that some Farmer will write unto me an Epistle saying, Thou art Weakly Sentimental; and if thou didst have to Re-Plant Corn four times by reason of the Robberies of the Crows, thou wouldst kill every Crow that the Lord delivered into thine hand. And I doubt not this is true. But he who holdeth in his hand a living thing that the Thorns have cruelly wounded must not be chided for his Compassion. And besides, there was Keturah, and she said to loose him and Let Him Go. 🙰

The
Unreckoned Gift

Now I had a friend, and his wife was a friend of Keturah; and he was a man who always had Misfortunes. And he came to me and said, Loan me an Hundred Dollars, and I will give thee my Note; yea, and I will pay thee Usury at the rate of Six Percent.

And I loaned him the Money, though I had need of it; and he paid me neither the Hundred Dollars nor the Usury. Yea, it was not according to his Principle to pay the Interest, neither was it to his Interest to pay the Principal. But whenever he met me, he made many Promises and many Apologies; and when his wife met Keturah, she was Embarrassed.

Now Christmas was approaching, and Keturah said, Let us Cancel that Note, and send it to them for Christmas. And I was Glad to Get Rid of it.

So I brought the note, and I sat me down, and I took my Pen and Mine Ink Horn, and I made figures.

And Keturah said, What doest thou, Safed?

And I said, I am computing the Interest; for it hath been Seven Years since this Note was given, and the Hundred Dollars hath become Two Hundred, or thereabout; and I would fain discern how much of a Gift we are making.

And Keturah said, Safed, I am ashamed of thee. Canst thou not do a Generous Deed without trying to Magnify it in thine own Imagination? Art thou not willing to give without Reckoning? Then thou knowest not the Real Joy of Giving. Yea, and thou reckonest wrongly. For what if thou shalt be able by computing and compounding Usury to make an Hundred Dollars into Two Hundred, still is thy gift not increased thereby. What thou art giving is not the money thou once didst loan, for that is gone, and the Note is not worth money; thou art giving Peace of Mind to thine unfortunate friend, and wiping the Blush of Confusion from the cheek of my friend. What that costeth us now is but a Scrap of Paper, but the value thereof cannot be reckoned in silver.

Now when I heard these things, I was pricked in mine heart. And I said, O my beloved, daughter of all the wisest of the angels, thy soul is a soul of pure gold, and thy speech is the voice of wisdom. Behold, some have called thy Husband a Generous Man, but thou art far more generous than I. For he who giveth and reckoneth hath still a Smirch of Stinginess in his Generosity; but thou givest and reckonest not; yea, and thus hast thou always given.

And I remembered these things, and I thought of the Good God, who giveth, and not according to measure. And I prayed, and I said, O, my God, forgive the Parsimony of our Generosity. ❧

The Procession
of the Years

There was a day when the Year was drawing nigh unto its end when I sat at the end of the day, and Keturah sat with me. And we spake of the Year that was nigh unto its ending, and of the number of the Years that had increased since first we knew each other. And we thought of the Toils and the Troubles and the Things that had Gone Wrong. And we spake of the War and of our sons who went forth unto what we knew not, and how they came again, but how the thing for which they fought still lingered and came not upon earth.

And we recalled by name the friends who had died, and the friends who had gone afar, and the friends of whom we have no present knowledge. And we thought of many things.

And I said, Keturah, it is harder to look a New Year in the face when one hath taken a careful look at the backs of so many Old Years. For I have seen few Old Years which men and women did not kick off the back step and slam the back door, while they hasted to the front door to welcome in a Year that was not better when it grew old.

But Keturah said, It is even so; and I have never wished to live over any of the Years that are past.

Nevertheless, I am glad of every one that I have lived, and I am thankful with each New Year that we still are living, and that we have courage and faith to face the unknown together.

And I said, Keturah, it is good to look back and to remember that among the many thousands of folk of all sorts and conditions that we have known, there have been few that wished to harm us, and many scores and even hundreds that would do us a kindness large or small. Yea, we have traveled together many years and in many lands, and have received few Curses and many Blessings, few Insults and many Words of Gratitude.

So we spake unto each other, and we called to mind the names and the faces of our friends, near and far, living and dead, and we were thankful for the Blessings of the Years.

And I said, Keturah, I miss the brown Curls that thou didst possess when first thou camest down the Pike toward me, and the Gossiping Angels were peeking out of Heaven to see how I should fall for thee. Verily, thou wert fair as the moon, clear as the sun, and terrible as an army with banners, and the Angels had no disappointment in the effect of thy vision upon me. But the grey hair is yet more beautiful, and the years that we live together grow better and better.

Now many other things we spake unto each other as we sat there together, on the Reviewing Stand of the New Year, and watched the procession of past Years receding and the dim Vision of Years to come, but what we said the one unto the other concerneth not any one of those who read this Parable. Save only that we face the Future with Undiminished Faith. ❧

Things Not
to be Forgotten

I rode upon a Railway Train, Somewhere in Kansas, and the Train stopped Thirty Minutes for Lunch. And at one end of the Station was there a little Park, with two great Sun Dials, whereof one showed Central Time and the other showed Mountain Time. And the Park was attractive, and had Cost the Railway Some Coin, and the result was worth it.

Now there stood in the little Park, hard by the Train, a strong White Post, as it were two cubits in height. And there was framed in the top of the post an old-time Drawbar, with a Coupling-Pin and a Link. And upon the Post was painted in Black Letters this Superscription, Lest We Forget.

And I said unto myself, It may be that this is the town where the man lived who first invented the Safety Coupler.

And I entered the Station, and I inquired of the Young Man who was Clerk of the Station Hotel. And I asked of him, saying,

Wherefore is that Post with the old Drawbar erected in this Town rather than in another?

And he said, Where is it at? For I have never seen it.

And I inquired of another, and he said,

Thou mayest search me; for I have never noticed it.

And I inquired of the Station Agent, and he said, I once knew, but, behold, I have forgotten.

Then did the Conductor say, All Aboard, and I got on board.

And I considered the days of my boyhood, when I played about the Cars, and I knew Railway workers; and many of them had lost fingers that were crushed in coupling cars; and many lost their hands, and others lost their lives.

And I said, Behold, there was one who considered all these things, and sat up nights, and peradventure pawned his Shirt that he might invent a method of avoiding all this. And here is his memorial, marked, Lest We Forget; and some pass it every day and never see it; and others once knew its meaning but they have forgotten.

And I looked out of the car window, and I beheld a Church, and upon the Church was a Spire, and upon the Spire was a Cross.

And I thought of the multitudes who continually pass it by, and I was grieved in mine heart; for I said, Among them are those who say, I have never seen it; and others say, I have seen it, but what it meaneth, behold, I know not. And others say, Behold, I once knew, but I have forgotten

Broadmoor Books are different. They are for the discriminating reader who admires fine writing and desires to be challenged by fresh and unconventional expressions of orthodoxy. Each book in this series has been chosen for its literary merit and imaginative appeal. Every effort has been made to achieve a high level of quality in design and production. Broadmoor Books aspire to be classics.

The text for *The Millionaire and the Scrublady* was set in 12-point Cochin with two points of leading. The typeface, adapted by Adrian Frutiger, was based on an eighteenth-century model. Cochin has a handsome, wide-set feel, and its matching italic is heavily scriptlike. The heads are set in Parsons Bold.

The compositor was Sue Koppenol of the Photocomposition Department of Zondervan Publishing House. The heads were set by the Composing Room of Grand Rapids, Michigan. The text was designed by Louise Bauer, and the cover was designed by Lecy Design of Minneapolis, Minnesota. The book was printed by Color House Graphics, Grand Rapids, MI on Weyerhaeuser 60 lb. Husky Vellum paper stock.